THE RAMBLER'S COMPANION

THE RAMBLER'S COMPANION

A Guide to the Countryside for Ramblers Cyclists & Motorists

by

HENRY GORDON

———◆———

Illustrated by

THERESA S. STANNARD

1937

CHATTO AND WINDUS

LONDON

PUBLISHED BY

Chatto & Windus

LONDON

*

The Macmillan Company
of Canada, Limited

TORONTO

FOREWORD

something of Nature's secrets, but who have not the time
nor the money to make a detailed study of it. If you are an
expert you will look in vain for any scientific
treatment here already described, and for that matter of

FOREWORD

I have lived in the country from boyhood until a few
years ago, when my work brought me into one of the
northern Home Counties. The prospect of becoming a
townsman frightened me, but I was fortunate enough to
secure a little place within twenty-five miles of London
which still remains rural. Here was peace indeed; not
another house in sight; water by windmill; entrancing
cherry orchards and walnut trees; but, above all, a still
unspoilt countryside, peopled by folk of the open air, as
simple as they were kind. I still remember our post-
woman, who for her honeymoon dared the first great
adventure of her life, and spent a day in London. Here life
still runs a quiet and even course in the absence of the
railway, but I am not going to tell you where to find this
harbour of rest.

Near our house a public footpath crossed the field, and
here in intervals of leisure I met and talked to my friends,
the ramblers. They came by twos and threes during the
week, but in great numbers over the week-ends. Although
they possessed one common desire for the open air and
exercise, I felt they often failed to obtain the maximum
benefits owing to lack of experience.

In the course of many conversations I discovered an
astounding desire for information about the natural
objects encountered by the way, and it was a source of
immense satisfaction to be able to tell them something
of our birds and flowers, and the little people inhabiting
the fields and hedgerows.

This little book is the result of our talks. It is designed
to help in a small way those thousands who wish to know

something of Nature's secrets, but who have not the time nor the money to make a detailed study of it. If you are an expert you will find many omissions; my schoolgirl daughter has already devastated me for the absence of any information on place-names and wasps. The difficulty has been, however, not what to put in, but what to leave out. In the hope that some may be led to inquire further, a bibliography of inexpensive books is given.

The marvels of Nature are in operation by day and night, and in all seasons. If you carry this small book in your pocket, and by its use identify a few unknown objects, and unravel an occasional mystery of the hedgerow and ditch, I shall be well satisfied.

I am deeply grateful to my many friends for their advice and encouragement, but particularly to that popular author Mr. A. G. Street, who with his unrivalled knowledge of practical farming has proved a most helpful critic; to Professor Salisbury; Captain St. Barbe Baker, Founder of the Men of the Trees; Professor Dawson, O.B.E.; Mr. L. Wynn Houghton, F.R.C.S.; Mr. Cecil Reeve, A.R.I.B.A., A.M.T.P.I., who have all given valuable time and counsel ungrudgingly and enabled me to compress the maximum amount of information in a minimum of space.

HENRY GORDON.

CONTENTS

Chapter I

PRACTICAL GUIDANCE FOR RAMBLERS

Section 1

WALKERS

(a) Care of Feet

Remember the success of your ramble depends funda-
mentally on the condition of your feet, and a blistered heel
will mar the enjoyment of the most perfect countryside.
Pay attention to three essentials and you will not experience any trouble.

(1) Select your footwear with care, as it is of first importance. You may wear either boots or shoes; it is a
matter for personal preference, but on no account should
they be too weighty, of hard leather, or heavily nailed.
Ladies will avoid much discomfort by using low heels.

(2) Socks or stockings should be woollen, of a reasonable thickness, and, above all, well fitting. If too short
they will form a lump under the foot, and if too long they
will make a crease at the back of the heel. Wrinkles and
big darns must be avoided. I do not recommend the practice of wearing a thin pair of socks under a thick pair of
stockings, and I have never found any benefit by rubbing
soap on the feet or socks. A word to the ladies—"Not silk
stockings, please."

(3) Cleanliness of the feet is important, and they should
be washed at least once a day on long walks. If you are on
a ramble of several days' duration, wash your feet as the
first job on arriving at your camp or hostel, dry them
afterwards thoroughly, and dust with talcum powder,

1

starch, or boracic powder. Put on dry socks, and wear slippers or canvas shoes during the evening. Excessive perspiration of the feet may be relieved by bathing them in a dilute solution of permanganate of potash. You require just enough to colour the water a clear red, and twopennyworth will last a long time. An alternative method, but to my mind not so satisfactory, is a solution containing a tablespoonful of formalin to a quart of water. I do not favour the use of methylated spirit for this purpose. If you are unfortunate enough after these precautions to get a blister, prick it with a clean needle. This can be sterilised over the flame of your spirit stove, or even in the flame of a match. Insert it gently under the skin on one side of the blister, push it through and bring it out on the other side, thus making two holes. A slight pressure will discharge all the fluid. The skin should not be removed, but fixed down with a piece of adhesive tape. In an emergency I have seen a postage stamp used for this purpose. If the skin does come off, cut away any ragged edges, smear with vaseline, and apply a small piece of gauze, fixed in position by adhesive tape. Corns cause great inconvenience. Temporary relief may be obtained by protecting the corn from the side of the boot by means of a small pad of cotton wool. Do not attempt to remove them with a razor blade or knife; there is always a risk of blood poisoning. Chiropodists will give you comfort and proper treatment at a very small cost. For home treatment get the following solution made up:

1 drachm of salicylic acid
20 grains of Indian hemp extract
1 fluid oz. of flexile collodion.

Paint this over the corn, and not the toe, for four or five nights, and then soak in very hot water. The great point with corns is to remove their cause. See that your boots fit properly, and remember that boots which are too large are as bad as those which are too tight. A final hint—keep your nails well cut and square.

(b) Equipment for Walkers

(1) *Clothing.* Personal inclination must always be the final factor in deciding on clothes for the rambler, but it is useful to bear certain points in mind, which are the result of long experience. For men, shorts or grey flannel slacks will be found the most comfortable. They must be cut full and not be too tight round the waist or chafe the legs. Avoid breeches and "plus fours." Braces are recommended instead of a belt to hold up shorts and slacks. They are not so smart it is true, but they allow more freedom, do not restrict the circulation, and prevent the shorts hanging low and chafing. See that all buttons are sewn on with strong thread. Open-neck shirts with a turn-down collar are most comfortable, and can be worn with a light, loose-fitting sports coat. A sleeveless open-neck pullover is useful in cold weather. Personally I do not favour a sweater. Retain your usual type of underclothing; it is folly to change to anything less substantial than you usually wear. A light raincoat or oilskin is essential. Avoid capes at all cost; they hamper the movements and allow the rain to drip on to the knees. If you must wear a hat, let it be of soft felt; the brim will protect you from sun and rain. I have found the canvas hats commonly used by rowing men the best proposition. They are light, inexpensive, fold easily into the pocket or pack, and have the necessary protective brim. On the other hand, if you prefer to go hatless, remember wet days, and keep a sou'-wester in your kit. The above remarks apply equally to ladies, with this exception, that a wide, well-cut skirt is preferable in every way to shorts or slacks. I have talked

to hundreds of ramblers on the point, and I have never yet found a lady who could honestly claim any advantage for men's apparel. In considering your clothes bear in mind:

(a) The season (hot or cold).

(b) The weather (wet or fine).

(c) Comfort and freedom.

(d) The duration of your ramble.

(e) The locality through which you intend passing.

(2) *The Rucksack or Pack*. The main point to bear in mind is never overload yourself, and observing this, a pack seems quite unnecessary for a day's ramble. If your lunch is bulky and you prefer to keep your pockets from bursting, a light haversack worn over the shoulder will meet all requirements. On the other hand, if you are sleeping out, the pack is essential. There are various kinds on the market, but when making your choice observe the following points, and insist on being fitted:

(a) Be reasonable in considering size. It is a temptation to allow for contingencies and select the biggest in the shop. You may bitterly regret this at the end of your first day. See that it is not too wide, like an exaggerated sack. It should, however, be long enough to fit into the curve of the body and ride on the back of the hips. Better too long than too short.

(b) Select a type that has one point of suspension from the centre of your shoulders, and not side suspension on the two carrying straps.

(c) Leather shoulder straps are preferable to webbing. They should be about two inches wide over the shoulder, but half that width under the arms.

(d) The material must be absolutely waterproof.

(e) Several outside pockets will be of more use than a

solitary big one. Make sure that the pocket flaps overlap well to keep out the rain.

(*f*) Army packs are cheap but not to be recommended, as they are too short and not comfortable to wear without the full equipment of belt and shoulder straps, which are not obtainable.

Many complain that a pack causes excessive perspiration on the back. I have seen this overcome by making a small framework composed of sections of sink cane and wire, and stitching this on to the pack where it meets the small of the back. The air can thus circulate, and the trouble is at any rate partly removed. It is possible for those who can afford it to buy a more elaborate type of this article, but the above answers very well. Some prefer to walk by day and put up at an inn at night. By doing this the amount to be carried is minimised. Here is a suggestion for the pack:

> Spare socks or stockings.
> Change of underclothing.
> Shirt.
> Canvas shoes.
> Holdall with washing and shaving kit and comb.
> Small piece of soap and solid tooth paste. (Avoid tubes of tooth paste or shaving cream.)
> Small mirror.
> Needles and thread and a piece of thick string.
> Spare laces.
> Towel.
> Enamel plate and mug, or billy can.
> Knife, fork and spoon.
> Electric torch.
> Candle and matches.
> Small bandage, sticking plaster and iodine.
> Small pair of scissors.

Penknife with tin-opener.

Boot-brush and cleaning material.

Handkerchiefs.

Pyjamas.

If you propose to sleep out, the following additions are advisable:

Good quality ground sheet. This must be absolutely waterproof.

Soft blanket with buttons and buttonholes to turn into a sleeping-bag if required. During the summer most people will find one blanket enough if they place a layer of newspaper inside. However, you must make your choice; if you are a cold mortal, you must carry more.

Good sweater.

Woolly cap. I find the best sleeping kit to be flannel trousers, socks and a sweater with a polo collar, but different ideas exist and you will ascertain from experience which suits you best.

Small tent. (See Camping Section p. 23.)

In addition some will wish to carry a camera (slung in case), map and compass, note-book, and perhaps a pocket copy of their favourite author. When packing, remember that the articles wanted last go at the bottom of the rucksack. Therefore pack in the reverse order required at night; blankets at the bottom, and mackintosh at the top in case of a sudden rainstorm. Do not carry your money loose, but in a leather purse in the back pocket of your slacks. If you have a button put on this pocket there is no possibility of the purse dropping out when you are lying on the ground.

Care of Boots

Squeaking Boots. Stand in sufficient linseed oil to just cover the soles for twenty-four hours. If this is not successful, a second treatment will remove all sound.

A Waterproof Black Boot Polish. Six ozs. of brown sugar candy dissolved in a little boiling water. Stir until the consistency of thick syrup and pour into a glazed earthenware jar. Add one oz. of each of the following:

Beeswax.

Indigo.

Ivory black.

2 ozs. of mutton fat freed from impurities by previously dissolving in boiling water and allowing to cool off.

2 ozs. soft soap.

Place the jar in a saucepan of boiling water, and heat until all the ingredients are melted, then stir in a quarter of a pint of turpentine and half an ounce of glycerine. Apply to the boots with a sponge or piece of cloth, and polish with soft rags.

Care of Thermos Flask

As soon as possible after use rinse out with cold water to which a little vinegar has been added, then invert in a cool place to drain, but do not insert the cork until the flask is in use again. It is a mistake to add milk to any liquid to be carried in a thermos flask, as no matter how carefully it has been cleaned afterwards, a smell of sour milk is bound to remain. Periodically pour into the flask a generous quantity of vinegar and one eggshell crushed into small pieces, and shake vigorously. Add a good quantity of warm water and shake again, then allow to stand for about an hour, after which shake again and rinse with cold water.

Section 2

CYCLISTS

In spite of the immense increase in motor cars and
motor cycles, and the cheap fare facilities of the railway
companies, the popularity of cycling remains.

It has many advantages when compared with other
forms of transport, the most important being that it is
cheaper and gives greater freedom in choice of route and
companionship. The cyclist is not restricted to a limited
radius like the pedestrian, and can choose the by-ways
which the motorist avoids. You may prefer to belong to
a club and join in communal runs, or your inclination
may be to go your own way with one or two well-chosen
companions.

Dress

The majority of cyclists prefer to go hatless in fine
weather, and to wear a shade over the eyes if the sun is
troublesome. In wet weather some use a skicap, but you
will find an oilskin sou'wester the best proposition in
every way. Fairly roomy plus fours are preferable to
shorts or slacks; avoid tight breeches at all costs. Try a
cricket shirt with open neck under a sports jacket instead
of a sweater. If you ride a sports machine, light cycling
shoes should be worn, but if you ride something heavier,
light shoes of any kind will meet the case. Boots are not
recommended, as they are too tight round the ankles and
produce soreness, if not blisters, on any long run.

The advantages of a good big cape in wet weather are
beyond dispute. It should be made of oilskin, light, and,
above all, roomy enough to go over the handlebars and
at the same time cover the pack, or the small of the back

if you are not carrying a pack. By the way, you may sometimes find it useful on a wet day to change your pack
round and carry it on your chest instead of on the back.
This obviates any difficulty if your cape is on the small
side, and can be done without inconvenience. Leggings
are not advised.

Choice of a Machine

Three types:

(a) *Road Racer*. We are not really concerned with
this machine, which is a lightweight built for fast
riding.

(b) *Sports Tourer*. This is equally light, but is built for
comfortable riding and is much favoured by those who
cover considerable distances in daily runs.

(c) *Roadster*. This is the ordinary type of cycle. The
frame is heavier, but it is the best machine for the serious
tourist who intends to carry a fair amount of kit.

A three-speed gear is not an absolute necessity, but
has much to recommend it. The disadvantage is that it is
difficult to repair if anything goes wrong, but trouble
should not arise if it is kept properly adjusted and oiled.
Always test before setting out on a long run.

A light chain case will increase the life of your chain.
This may be either dust-excluding or oil-retaining, and
the former will be found the most satisfactory.

Brakes are most important. Remember that you are
required by law to have two brakes in good working
order. Sports models are fitted with caliper brakes
adapted to the special type of Endrick rims on these
machines. These brakes are worked by a cable. Roadsters,
on the other hand, have two rim brakes working off levers
fitted parallel to the handlebars. An internal expanding
hub brake is also on the market. It is of course not affected

2

by wet weather, but the inside of the drum must be kept free from oil.

The saddle is most important. It should have a wide back narrowing to the front, and should be fairly hard but well sprung. Avoid saddle covers, but occasionally dress the under side with saddle soap or some preservative. A point to remember is that if the saddle is too wide in front it may chafe your legs.

Solid rubber pedals are a comfort. Do not use toe clips.

If you use an oil lamp, it should be a good one. An electric lamp is handy, but you must remember always to carry a spare battery and bulb. I do not favour the dynamo type of lamp. You are required by law to carry a red rear reflector, and at least six square inches of white on your rear mudguard, but a small electric red lamp is a great additional safeguard and well worth the little extra expense involved.

The best tyres are the most economical in the long run.

Every cyclist must carry some audible warning device. A good bell of the lever and hammer type is still the best for this purpose.

Verify before starting that your tool bag is complete. There is no necessity to take a workshop, but the following are essential:

> Three tyre levers.
> Adjustable spanner.
> Spanners to fit all nuts.
> Cone spanner.
> Small screwdriver.
> Complete repair outfit with spare valve rubbers and
> brake blocks.
> Oil can with lubricating oil.
> Spare battery and bulb if your lamp is electric.
> Good pump.

Carrying Kit

Many still wear the rucksack, and if you propose to do this, hang it low so as to gain support from your luggage carrier. Do not allow it to hang down without a luggage carrier, as the weight may be too much for your back mudguard. There are other methods, however, for carrying kit which are to be preferred. Large-size cycling bags can be purchased to attach to the back of the saddle, and these hold a surprising amount if carefully packed. They usually contain outside pockets to hold the tools.

If you are camping and have a good deal of kit, large rectangular bags can be bought from any good stores. These bags are attached to the carrier and hang down one on each side of the rear wheel, leaving additional space on the carrier. Two old army packs answer the purpose equally well, providing they are securely fixed. Your cape should always be strapped on to the outside in order to be immediately available in case of a storm. Pack the things you require frequently on top. See that everything is strapped securely, and carry your gear as far as possible lengthwise to avoid wind resistance. Do not carry more than is absolutely necessary. Many a day has been ruined by overloading. In fact, unless you are camping, why not limit yourself to sandwiches and have your lunch in the open ? Go in somewhere and have a good tea, but select a place not more than fifteen miles from home, as it is depressing to contemplate an extended run at the end of the day.

Some Useful Hints

Have a cyclometer if you wish, but avoid too many gadgets. In the long run they mean more trouble.

Keep your tyres properly inflated, and as hard as is

comfortable. In icy weather let out a little air; it will help them to grip the slippery road surface.

Do not ride in the middle of the road, but keep about three or four feet from the side. This is safe, and you will avoid punctures from the flints in the gutter.

Do not try and ride every hill; it is bad for both you and the machine.

Never ride more than two abreast.

If a motorist sounds his horn and the road is clear, signal him on.

Remember you use the same signs as a motorist, and should give a clear indication of your intentions.

If your wheel becomes out of true, get it adjusted by some reputable shop, as it is a difficult job for an amateur.

If your back tyre is worn, change it over with the front tyre, and remember to pick out flints frequently.

Bearings should be inspected every few months. Even if only one is worn or damaged, get a new set.

The chain should be well lubricated. Take it off periodically, clean thoroughly in petrol, and wipe on a graphite lubricant before replacing. The chain must not be too tight, and there should be between a half to one inch play when it is fixed.

Be courteous to other road users, and err always on the side of safety.

Section 3

THE COMPASS, MAP READING AND DIRECTION FINDING

The Compass

A compass is not strictly necessary if your course lies along the sign-posted roads, but you will find it invaluable if your route is across the moors or open country. The instrument is familiar to all and can be purchased quite cheaply. It consists of a circular card, on which are marked the four cardinal points—North, East, South and West—all of which are joined. The circle is thus divided by four lines of ninety degrees each, and the four sections thus formed are again sub-divided into North-East, South-East, South-West and North-West. The compass contains a far greater number of divisions, but for the purpose on hand eight are sufficient. A delicate needle is mounted on a pivot at the centre of the circle, and this, being magnetised, always points to the magnetic north, or magnetic pole, and not to the true north as indicated by the Pole Star. The difference between the two is called the variation, and differs with each place.

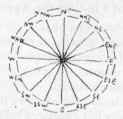

To Set a Map by Compass

All good maps have two arrow lines on them, showing the true north and the magnetic north. It will probably be necessary to extend these lines a few inches by pencil marks. Then place the compass on them and turn the map gently round until the north point of your compass lies on the north point of the map; the needle will also be along the magnetic north line on the map, which is now set in the correct direction.

For walking you will find the Ordnance Survey, or maps based on the Survey, and on a scale of one inch to a mile, most useful. See that they are mounted on linen.

To Set a Map without a Compass

Stand on some definite spot marked on the map, then identify a distant object on the map and join the two points with a straight pencil line. Turn the map about the point on which you stand until it lies in the direction of the distant object. Your map is now set.

There is an alternative method which can be adopted when you cannot determine your own position exactly. Identify two distant points on either side of you and join them by a straight pencil line on the map. Then revolve the map until the line points in the direction of your two marks on the landscape.

Two Methods of Finding the Approximate North

(a) *By Day*. Assuming that your watch is correct, point the hour hand directly at the sun, and the south will be midway between an angle formed by the hour hand and twelve o'clock; the north will, of course, be in exactly the opposite direction.

(b) *By Night*. In the British Isles look for the Great Bear in the sky, which is illustrated below.

The two stars on the outside edge of the saucepan point to the bright Pole Star, which is approximately north. Remember, however, that the Great Bear revolves round the Pole, and will appear sometimes upside down.

To Tell the Time by Compass

The sun rises in the east, sets in the west, and is south at midday. With this information in your mind, you can approximate the time by its position between your fixed points of east, south and west.

Scales

The scale of a map is a measurement of a length on the map compared with the same distance on the land it represents. Maps on which one inch represents one mile of country are the most useful. You will find the scale in words at the bottom of the map, and, for example, in the one-inch scale you may notice under the words a line divided up into five inches, representing five miles. The first section is sub-divided in ten sections, each of which represents one-tenth of a mile. The use of the scale is now obvious. Mark off the distance between your required points and place it against the scale, and you can read it in miles. The scales vary, and on big maps may be as much as twenty-five inches to the mile, or on very small maps one inch to ten miles.

Contour Lines

The map maker has had to discover a method of showing rises and depressions in the ground, and if you can read a map properly you will be able to determine at a glance whether a distant object is concealed by an intervening hill or out of sight in a hollow. This is done by thin wavy lines, red on Ordnance maps, which join up all points of equal height above sea-level. Look at your map and trace them round; the actual height is clearly shown by small figures. If the contours are drawn close together, the slope will be steep, but if spread out and some distance apart, the slope will be gentle.

Conventional Signs

In order to show the various features of the countryside clearly a series of conventional signs has been devised, a key to which is usually given at the bottom of the map. It shows different objects by some simple, easily recognised sign. For example, a church with a tower is depicted by a small black square surmounted by a cross; a church with a spire, by a small black ring crowned by a cross; a church without tower or spire, by a simple cross. Find these various signs on your map and memorise them. In other maps letters may be used as signs. They are self-evident—for example, Sch. School, B. Bridge.

Section 4

CLOUDS AND WEATHER FORECASTING

Have you ever spent a lazy hour on a summer afternoon, with nothing particular to do and with your thoughts drugged by the warm air, the scent of flowers, perhaps the drone of the bee or the song of the skylark? In such a mood the mind does not register details but impressions. Not infrequently these may be nothing more than a sense of humility, caused by the immensity and grandeur of some great white, billowy cloud, standing like a silent sentinel in the blue sky. If this impassive giant should change almost imperceptibly, and develop darker clouds at its base, the effect on the mind is singular, because gradually, almost as though awakening, you become apprehensive. You have sensed a change in the clouds without perhaps realising that their formation has changed, or indeed that they had any special form.

Clouds vary considerably, and may be classified

according to their shape, size, colour and altitude into four main divisions.

Cirrus, or curl clouds (altitude 30,000 feet), may be identified in the first place by their great height. They are

of a white feathery appearance, sometimes like a colossal lock of hair blown by the wind and extending right across the sky.

Cumulus, or cotton-wool clouds (altitude 4000–6000 feet), are the great white, billowy clouds of summer. If

they are opposite the sun, their surface shows some shadows, but is brighter than the edges. If they are on the same side as the sun, they have a dark appearance, with brilliant, almost incandescent margins.

Nimbus, or rain clouds (altitude 6000 feet), are thick layers of dark cloud without shape, and with ragged edges, from which continuous rain falls.

Stratus (altitude 3000 feet) is simply a horizontal sheet of lifted fog.

When these main forms have been broken up, but still retain their general characteristics, the word "fracto" should precede the cloud name. For example, the small loose rain clouds travelling at high speed at low levels are called fracto-nimbus; the giant cumulus, when broken into numerous smaller woolpacks, takes the name fracto-cumulus.

It is obvious that the constantly changing winds will cause various combinations of the four main forms, and these are shown in the table below. These forms can be sub-divided again, but space will not permit the minute details of description necessary to identify them.

A. Upper Clouds (altitude 30,000 feet).

1. Cirrus.

2. Cirro-stratus. A thin white sheet of cloud of great horizontal depth, sometimes covering the sky, but only giving it a whitish appearance.

B. Intermediate Clouds (altitude 16,000 feet).

3. Cirro-cumulus. Clouds broken up into small fleecy masses, often appearing in lines or groups. These

clouds have only very slight shadows, or may have none.

4. Alto-cumulus. Closely packed, curved white clouds, arranged in lines—mackerel sky.

5. Alto-stratus. Similar to cirro-stratus, but only half the height.

C. Lower Clouds (altitude 6000–7000 feet).

6. Strato-cumulus. Large globular masses of dark cloud, frequently covering the whole sky. Not very thick, and often showing patches of blue sky through its intervening spaces. Similar to nimbus, but it is globular in appearance and does not bring down rain.

7. Nimbus.

D. 8. Cumulus (altitude 4000–6000 feet).

9. Cumulo-nimbus. Have the form of cumulus but are dark at the base, from which local rainstorms will fall. Above these you will frequently see a sheet of fibrous clouds.

E. 10. Stratus (altitude 3000 feet).

Weather Forecasting

Weather forecasting is now performed scientifically, and with great accuracy. Ramblers will find the barometer and the wireless forecasts of considerable assistance.

There are, however, many natural signs, based on the experience of those who live open-air lives, which indicate the weather possibilities, some for a few hours, some for a day ahead. These are not, of course, infallible, but are of general accuracy. One may fail you, but a combination of several should be fairly safe. Try these out for yourself over a period of six months, recording your successes and failures.

Fine weather indications:

When the smoke from chimneys rises steadily in a straight line.

Marigold blossoms are open widely in the morning.

If the scarlet pimpernel remains open, even on a cloudy morning.

Heavy dews at night during the summer.

Larks fly high and sing continuously when in the air.

Gnats fly in large numbers in the evening.

Beetles and bats fly late in the evening.

Numerous spiders' webs in the hedgerows.

Moon very clear and bright.

If bees are about—they are never caught in the rain.

Indications of rain:

If chimney smoke blows downwards.

If the setting sun on the previous night is pale.

The sun setting behind a heavy bank of clouds after a fine day.

The moon with a halo round it.

Bats squeaking on the wing.

An unusual clearness in the atmosphere, making distant objects appear nearer than usual.

Spiders idle in their webs.

Rooks returning to their rookeries before their accustomed time, or not flying far during the day.

Gulls flying inland.

Swallows flying low and skimming over the surface of the ground.

Donkeys braying.

Cattle assembling at a corner of the field with their tails to the windward.

Cattle and sheep lying about in the fields for hours, in preference to being on their feet.

Other Hints

When the wind blows from the sun all day—that is from the east in the morning and west in the evening—you may be fairly certain of fair, dry weather. Should the wind suddenly change and blow from the west in the morning and east in the evening, rain may be expected on the following day.

Remember: Wind with the sun all day—fine.

Against the sun all day—wet.

Thunderstorms will soon pass if they come up with the wind, but they will last longer and be more severe if they come up against the wind.

A south-west wind generally means rain.

Rabbits feed early if a rainy night is coming.

Section 5

CAMPING

Most people have an ambition to camp at some time in their lives; some achieve it through force of circumstances and lose their enthusiasm; some take to it like a duckling to water, and almost evolve a craft of their own by building a wide personal experience into an edifice of first principles. These brief notes are not for such experts, but are intended for those who entertain the pious wish to live and sleep in the open air for a brief period between the more exacting duties of life, and either do not know how or fear to take the initial step.

A popular theory exists that camping is uncomfortable, involving sleepless nights, indifferent food and a continuous round of dish washing, wood chopping and hard grinding work. It can be so, but there is no reason why it should if you "plan ahead." This is of fundamental importance, and no detail should be too small for consideration before starting. As you grow more experienced this planning will become a habit and automatic, and you will not experience discomfort, but learn for the first time in your life, perhaps, the joy of complete freedom. You will not be restricted to the road, or by considerations of time or place, unless you have not "planned ahead" and have to traverse an additional five miles to obtain something important which you have forgotten.

You will find information on personal equipment, cooking and fire making in other sections of this book, and these notes will deal therefore with sleeping arrangements, and the construction and management of the camp.

One-Night Camp

We deal in the first place with the one-night, movable camp, which is set up in the evening and moved on the following morning when your journey is resumed.

Site. The site of your camp is important. Be sure and select a spot which is protected from adverse weather, preferably on the sheltered side of a wood or copse, as nothing is so disconcerting as a heavy wind. Do not actually pitch in the wood, but a few yards from the verge. Examine the ground and make sure that it is fairly level, dry and not boggy. It is an advantage to be reasonably near a stream, both for cooking and ablution purposes. Avoid the proximity of a pond, which may be the breeding-ground of mosquitoes. Ask yourself "Where is the nearest dwelling?" It is not a disadvantage if one is in the vicinity. Presumably they have supplies of milk and eggs for themselves, and may augment your own larder if necessary. The final question before getting to work is whether you are on private ground or not, and if you are, whether you have obtained permission to camp. Always do this when possible; you will seldom be met with a refusal, and at any rate you will be relieved of any possibility of being "moved on."

Shelter. A few veterans and a host of beginners will bivouac in the open, with a ground sheet and blanket only; the former because they prefer it, and the latter because they do not know any better. Do not attempt it, because such a method is uncomfortable and unnecessary except on the warmest nights. One school of thought favours the waterproof sleeping bag, with an extension from the head to form a roof; but it is not recommended, as not only is it heavy, but very restricted in space. Confinement in such a shelter on a wet night would be enough to test the enthusiasm of the keenest camper. There is only one really satisfactory form of shelter, and that is a small tent. In view of the fact that it has to be carried, either on your back or on your bicycle, it must not only be extremely light, but also waterproof and capable of easy erection. There are various inexpensive types which can be examined at any big store, and you will be guided by your own personal ideas to some extent. It will perhaps help if you bear in mind a few points. In the first place, do not attempt to make your own tent, as there is only a very remote possibility of it being satisfactory, and there will be little saving in cost, if any. First examine the material. There are two essentials: it must be light and it must be waterproof; therefore discard heavy canvas and select a light material which is closely woven. Few people will wish to undertake a ramble solo, but if you are one of these rare but quite understandable folk, avoid any but the most simple tent. You will find the type fitted with a single extending bamboo pole and one guy rope

easy to erect and dismantle. This is important, as you will
not want to spend a long time on this business at the end
of a day's walking. If you ramble with a companion,
it is possible to be a little more ambitious in the matter of
your shelter. Select a one-roofed tent, just big enough to
hold you both. It should be of the two-poled pattern,
fitted with bamboos, but these can be dispensed with if
you cut your staffs to the required length and use them to
support the tent. Do not be persuaded into buying a
double-roofed tent or other extras, as they all have to be
carried. One last point, make sure that the sides will be
fairly steep when the tent is erected, as this will facilitate
the water running off and stop dripping. If the pitch of
the roof is too flat, it may give you a little more room
inside, but you will suffer for it in rain.

Your Bed. The ground sheet is the basis on which the
bed is made. It must be absolutely waterproof and light,
but not too small. A large pair of lightweight, warm
blankets are ideal, although some take only one made up
into the form of a sleeping bag. The first point to remember is that it is essential to have as much clothing underneath as on top, and you will sleep cold or probably not
sleep at all unless you bear this in mind. Lay your ground
sheet out in the tent and spread the first blanket with one
edge resting on the left-hand edge of the ground sheet—
being double the size of the ground sheet, the width
will, of course, lie right across the tent. Next lay some
newspaper on the blanket above the ground sheet and
spread your second blanket with its edge lying over the
right-hand side of the ground sheet. Pull this blanket
over double, lay a few sheets of newspaper on top, and
double your first blanket in the same manner. Tuck the
end in underneath, fasten with a large safety pin, and you
have a comfortable draughtproof bed. If you are travelling

light, with one blanket made up as a sleeping bag, remember to put plenty of newspaper underneath, and do not disdain your mackintosh on top providing it is dry. A good pillow will ensure a good night's rest. Spend a little time on this, and experiment until you evolve something to suit. Some people carry a small bag of about eighteen inches by twelve, which they fill with leaves. This is an excellent notion providing they are reasonably dry. In addition, use your pack, spare clothes, and build up to the required height.

Water. Where possible, obtain your water from some recognised source of supply, but if this is not possible, use a running stream, having satisfied yourself that there is no reason to suspect its purity. Rain water can be used if fresh, but avoid ponds at all cost. It is most important to remember that you cannot judge water by sight, taste and smell. Water which looks quite safe may contain disease germs, and the only safeguard is to boil before drinking.

Latrine. For one night it is not necessary to dig an elaborate latrine, but you should certainly follow the general principle and bury; a depth of six inches is quite sufficient.

On Departure. Do please leave the camping site in the same condition as you found it. Everything combustible should be burnt, and anything which will not burn, buried. Verify that your fire is out before leaving.

The Standing Camp

The general principles applicable to a standing camp are much the same as for a one-night camp; the details only differ.

Nothing need be added to the previous notes on a choice of site, but if you are staying more or less

3

permanently you will not be so troubled over the weight
of your equipment and will choose something more substantial and roomy in the way of tents. There is a good
deal to be said for the bell tent, as it provides a roomy
shelter. It will take three beds comfortably, and if you
require space for numbers, six or eight can sleep quite
easily on the ground. A bell tent is not difficult to put up
providing one of the recognised methods is adopted. If
you have to pitch the tent, try this. Select a level piece
of ground, observing the hints on sites, and mark the
centre position of the tent by driving in a peg, and mark
off a circle by attaching a piece of string about four yards
long. Choose a spot on the lee side where the door is to be,
and make a heel mark; about half a yard on each side of
this put in two pegs on the circumference of your circle.
Put two further pegs in roughly a similar position on the
other side of the circle. Now open the tent with the door
opposite the heel mark, slip the pole into the cap of the
tent and raise it into an upright position. While it is thus
held, a second person should slip the guy ropes on to the
pegs. The tent will now stand without being held. Lace up
the door in order to prevent the opening being stretched
too far. Now go round and insert further pegs on the
circle and attach guy ropes, tightening them slightly.
Open the door and insert the brailing pegs into the loops
at the bottom of the wall.

Dig a shallow trench about six inches deep and nine
inches wide round the tent, but carrying it away to the
side before you reach the door to take off any accumulated
water. Dig a small hole about six inches deep by the side
of your tent pole, which can be moved into it to lessen
strain if a sudden storm falls.

Some will, however, prefer the wall tent on account of
the ridge giving more ventilation. There are many

varieties, some with a fly-sheet or extra roof. Examine them at the store, and select according to your purse.

General Hints. Thoroughly air the tent every day, and if the weather is fine, turn out the contents into the sun. Roll up all bedding, and keep the inside tidy. Slacken guy ropes in wet weather, but tighten them in wind.

The camp kitchen has been dealt with in another section, but no apology is needed to emphasise again the importance of cleanliness and tidiness. All rubbish should be put in your rubbish pit, and if there are more than two or three campers, it is advisable to have a wet pit, or soakaway for your greasy water. Washing water may be thrown away, but if you do this with greasy water, flies will soon assemble.

Latrines should be situated in a discreet position some distance to the east of your tents if possible. Nothing elaborate is required. Remove the turf and roll it up for replacement later, and dig a narrow trench three feet long by one foot wide by nine inches deep. Heap the earth up at the side for covering purposes, which must be considered of first importance.

In a fixed camp, beds will probably be used instead of sleeping on the ground. The ordinary camp bed is cheap and convenient if you have means of transport to get it to the camp. Some very good waterproof mattresses can be bought quite cheaply, or an old army valise is very comfortable and will keep you warm below. A final suggestion is a cotton palliasse stuffed with straw, if you can get it near at hand, or alternatively, with dry leaves and bracken. Two blankets should suffice.

Section 6

COOKING

Cooking in the open is an easy matter for the old hand, but it occupies a certain amount of time, and experience is necessary. The reader may not have these essential factors at his disposal, and he is therefore given, unblushingly, alternatives which may well be scoffed at by those who would play the backwoodsman in the by-lanes of the Home Counties.

One-Day Rambles

Presumably you wish to travel light, without the encumbrance of a pack; in addition, the time at your disposal is limited. Lunch at some wayside inn is not to be despised, but the majority will prefer a meal in the open. This can be carried in a light haversack, which will hold all required for a day. Humble bread and cheese is sustaining, but most people will prefer something more tasty, and to them sandwiches may form the base of the meal. There is no need to limit these to meat. Have you ever thought of the following: egg and cress; cucumber; cream cheese and chopped gherkins; eggs and capers; mashed eggs with a little curry powder and cress; grated cheese mixed to a paste with a little vinegar and butter; sardines and tomatoes; potatoes well flavoured with pepper and salt; bananas; raisins and nuts. A little watercress or lettuce carried in skinproof paper improves the sandwiches.

As an alternative, you may prefer bread and butter with hard-boiled eggs and tomatoes; cold sausages; or hard-boiled eggs cut in half and the yolk mixed with sardines

and replaced, the egg afterwards being wrapped in a
lettuce leaf.

For a sweet, try a piece of cold bread pudding, a Ban-
bury cake, or garibaldi biscuits with chocolate. Bananas
and apples are always a standby.

It seems hardly necessary to carry anything to drink,
as this can be obtained quite easily when required.

If you insist on tea in the open, carry a thermos flask.
You will learn, however, that the better method is to
select some congenial tea garden, according to your
means and inclination, not too far from your railway
station, or destination if you are not returning by train.
Have your tea at leisure, rest, talk, and then complete the
final stage of your ramble refreshed and at peace with the
world.

Moving Camps

You will certainly wish to do your own cooking in a
ramble of several days' duration. The first essential is the
ability to make a good fire out of the materials at hand. In
this connection always obtain permission to use the
camping site and make fires, as failure to do so is not only
discourteous, but liable to cause you much personal
inconvenience if difficulty arises when your camp is set.

Obviously your fire will be near your tent, and it is
hoped you will select a sheltered spot. The actual site
for the fire should be away from bushes and overhanging
branches. If possible, it should be free of grass and twigs,
and dried leaves should be cleared by sweeping a stick
round on the surface of the ground. These precautions
minimise the risk of the fire breaking bounds and getting
out of control.

On the other hand, the location of your fire depends on
your camp, and not your camp on the fire. You may

therefore have to build it sometimes on grass. When this is so, cut away two or three turves and roll them up ready to replace when you leave.

First collect your kindling wood. I believe birch bark is the standard recommendation for this purpose, and certainly it is good. The birch sheds its bark in thin loose strips, which can be removed from the trunk without difficulty. If the piece selected adheres tightly to the tree, damage may be done by removing it. However, you will not always have birch trees at hand, but safe and certain kindling may be gathered in the form of dead twigs from the bottoms of hedges or bushes, dead gorse, fir cones, or really dry bracken; use the latter sparingly.

Be sure and obtain an ample supply of wood before applying the match, and arrange in two heaps: kindling for ignition, and stouter sticks for keeping a sustained heat.

Fuel must be selected carefully. Ash is the only satisfactory wood to burn green, but dead wood from the following can be recommended: pine, fir, larch, birch, beech, oak, sycamore, holly and hazel. Remember touchwood or rotten wood is useless, and will only smoulder. Avoid elm, chestnut, elder and poplar.

Every one has his own particular system for building a fire. Try the following, and then evolve your own plan:

(1) For a small fire in quiet weather use a handful of kindling with some dry sticks on top. Apply a match to the kindling and feed twig by twig until going well; then add larger sticks one by one until the fire is of the size required. Remember to keep it as small as possible for the purpose for which it is intended.

(2) Place a small heap of kindling on the ground. Lay a number of dry sticks horizontally on top with further rows crossing them. Ignite on the windward side, and

feed until a good heap of hot ashes is formed, which will keep the fire going.

(3) Sharpen one end of a stick, and then, commencing about three inches from the point, slice the stick towards the other end, without actually shaving the slices off, and bend them out at right angles. Place the stick with the pointed end in the ground and arrange kindling round it. Tie dry twigs into bundles with grass and lean these bundles against the upright. Stouter sticks can be placed over the twigs, the whole forming a small pyramid. Ignite to the windward, and feed slowly with bigger stuff until well alight.

Assuming the fire burning satisfactorily, your next problem will be cooking.

The dingle-stick idea is simple and effective. Insert a stout stick in the ground at an angle and at a short distance from the fire, so that the end will bend over immediately above it. Place a large stone on the fire side of the stick to act as a support when the stick is bent, and hang your kettle or can on the end as near the top of the fire as possible.

The Tripod. Tie three stout sticks of equal length together in the form of a tripod, and suspend the can over the fire, low enough to be actually in the flames. If this turns out to be your usual method, it might be worth while to carry a small hook or piece of wire in your haversack. Failing this you can cut a very satisfactory hook from the hedge by selecting a short straight piece of branch about six inches long with smaller forked branches growing from opposite sides at each end. Shorten these to about two inches from the main piece, and you will have a very serviceable hook.

Another Method. Place stones or turves on either side of the fire to support the can, or alternatively, scrape a narrow channel in the ground in which the fire is built, but remember the sides must be kept sufficiently close to bear the can.

If you are cycling or have the means of carrying a Primus stove, you can save a good deal of trouble in fire building, but your cooking will be limited to boiling, frying, and in some circumstances stew. Some experts may scoff at the idea, but it has much to commend it.

The black from the smoke can be removed from your tins quite easily if they are slightly greased outside before use.

The Standing Camp

The cooking arrangements in a standing camp are on the same lines as those for a one-night stay, but need more organisation.

Your fires will be bigger and you will therefore need more wood. This should be sorted and piled neatly into heaps—small, medium and large. The larger pieces of wood are required for keeping in the fire, but you must have a supply of the small materials to restore a dying fire. An accumulation of hot ashes is important for baking, and many other purposes which practice will teach you.

Although the fires will be bigger, the principles of building and lighting are the same.

The Pole Fire. Instead of building in a heap arrange your sticks lengthwise, say two to three feet long; this will enable you to use two or three pots at the same time by the dingle-stick method.

The Shallow Trench Fire can be utilised to advantage, but it should be deeper and longer: deeper to accumulate the hot ashes, and longer to take more than one cooking can. An alternative to this method is to arrange rows of turves or two logs with the fire between them.

Water should always be available, and the bucket might be hung conveniently out of the way of clumsy feet, which otherwise might have disastrous effects on the fire.

Newspaper, earth and wood ash are wonderful for removing grease or egg from knives, forks and utensils before actually washing them. If you remember this, you will save some very greasy jobs.

Do not scatter debris about, but have a small pit near by, and cover all rubbish with a layer of earth—flies breed quickly.

It is always advisable to let one person be responsible for the cooking and tidiness of the camp kitchen.

Large oval toffee tins make excellent cooking utensils.

Frying. This is the quickest and most convenient method of outdoor cookery.

Bacon will fry in its own fat, and the same generally applies to sausages, although as a safeguard it might be as well to put a small piece of butter in the pan before frying sausages. The same may be said to apply to steak or chops.

Eggs, tomatoes and bacon may all be cooked in the same pan, but remember to put the tomatoes in first, then the eggs, and finally the bacon, as the latter cooks much more rapidly. Onions take a time to fry.

Potatoes require to float in deep fat, and are therefore not always convenient in camp. Packets of potato crisps can be bought. They are carried easily and add to the enjoyment of a meal if warmed before serving.

Apple Fritters. Make a thick paste of flour, egg and milk. Cover your apple slices with this and fry.

Scrambled Egg and Tomato. Beat up an egg with a little milk and some shredded tomato. Add pepper and salt, and place in a greased pan over the fire. Serve when set.

Time taken to fry:

Bacon	..	..	..	2 minutes
Eggs	..	..	..	2–3 minutes
Fritters	..	..	..	2–3 minutes
Sausages		..	..	5 minutes
Potatoes	..		..	5–6 minutes
Tomatoes		..	..	5 minutes
Steak	..	..	..	10 minutes

Stewing. A stew is an economical meal, but it takes a long time to cook, and this is sometimes a serious consideration when deciding on the menu. Good beef or mutton is the best foundation. If uncooked it will take twice as long as cooked meat. Cover the meat with water, taking care not to have too much liquid, and bring nearly to the boil. Skim fat off the surface, add onions, potatoes, carrots, peas, or any vegetable available. Be careful to allow to simmer and not to boil for two hours, watching to see it does not burn.

Stewed apples are a quick dish. Peel and slice, add a little water and sugar, and allow to simmer for a few minutes.

Roasting. Meat can be roasted over the fire by either suspending it or holding smaller pieces on a peeled green stick.

Potatoes can be baked in the hot ashes.

Pastry Stumps. Make a thick dough of flour, water and baking powder. Divide up and place round, and three or four inches along, a green stick. Bake over the fire, withdraw stick, and eat with jam, butter or cheese.

Boiling. Boil potatoes in their skins after scrubbing them. A very palatable soup can be made from packet soups, which are cheap and easy to carry.

Section 7

DISTANCE JUDGING

The ability to judge distance with reasonable accuracy will yield the rambler much pleasure and entertainment, and may in some circumstances prove extremely useful.

The average untrained eye is quite incapable of judging even short distances, but practice and the knowledge of a few elementary rules will effect a marked and rapid improvement.

Experience has shown that it is impossible to gauge with any marked degree of accuracy any distance above 1500 yards; beyond this you can estimate only. In the first stage of your experiment you might profitably limit your efforts up to half a mile, and proceed to longer distances only when you become proficient in the shorter ones. It is important to develop your powers of observation, as guessing is useless, and judging imperative with some good reason for your conclusion.

Some Simple Methods

1. *Unit System*. Measure out a short distance, say 100 yards; if you have not got a measure make it 120 paces, which will be near enough. Familiarise yourself with this thoroughly, if possible at different times of the day, in sunshine and in cloudy weather. Later apply the known distance to the object you are judging. How many times will the familiar 100 yards fit into the distance in question?

2. *By the apparent Size and Visibility of the Object, if its Size is known*. For this purpose you can use a man, a horse, a cow, doors, windows, or indeed anything of a standard size. It is useless to employ trees and similar

things, which are variable in height. To a person of average eyesight, the mouth and eyes of a man can be clearly seen at 50 yards, but at 100 yards they appear as points only. All parts of a man's body can be easily distinguished at 200 yards. The outline of his face becomes blurred at 300 yards, while at 400 yards it disappears, leaving only the outline of the body. Movements of the arms and legs can still be seen at 500 yards, but cease at 600 yards, when the head is barely visible. From 700 yards upwards a man is no longer evident as such, but appears as a mere shapeless object.

You will probably over-estimate distance in dull and misty weather, or in the evening; in very hot weather, when the heat rising from the ground produces a visible movement in the air; when the object is against a background of similar colour, or is in the shade; in looking across a valley or over broken country; when the object is at the end of a long avenue of trees.

You will probably under-estimate distance if the air is bright and clear, or the sun is shining behind you; when the object is against a background of a different colour; when looking upwards, downwards, or across level ground.

3. *Average Method.* Judge the maximum distance, then the minimum distance to the object, and take the average.

Rest on some well-defined spot which permits a good view of the surrounding countryside. Judge the distance to a number of conspicuous spots and record this on paper. Then measure these distances on your map, and using the scale, check off against your estimate. Practise frequently, and you will be surprised at the improvement made.

Section 8

KNOTS

In camp, on rambles, or even in your own home, it is of great importance to be able to tie certain elementary "knots" with speed and accuracy, using either cord or rope.

You will find the descriptive instructions easier to understand if you are familiar with the following definitions:

A knot is formed on the cord itself, generally at the end to form a stop.

A bend is the method of fastening or tying two cords together.

A hitch is the method of securing to a pole or spar.

A seizing is the way of fastening two poles together by a rope, or two ropes by a third.

The standing part of a cord or rope is the main portion, and sometimes the fixed part.

A bight is the loop formed while tying.

(1) *Overhand Knot.* Used to make a stop or prevent the end from fraying. It is made by passing the loose end A round the other end B and through the resultant loop.

(2) *Bowline.* Is a loop which will not slip at the end of a rope. Place the end A over the standing part B. Form with B a bight C over A. Take A round behind B and through the bight C.

(3) *Reef Knot.* Is used to join two ropes together or for bandaging. Place left end over right and turn under, then turn right end over left, turn through loop and pull.

(4) *Half Hitch.* Is used to secure the ends of cords to

OVERHAND   BOWLINE (I)   BOWLINE (2)   BOWLINE (3)

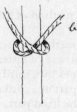

REEF
KNOT

HALF
HITCH

CLOVE
HITCH (I)

CLOVE
HITCH (2)

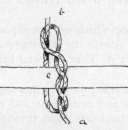

SHEEP-
SHANK

TIMBER HITCH

FISHERMAN'S
BEND

spars or sticks. Pass the end A of a rope round the standing part B, and through the bight.

(5) *Clove Hitch*. Used for the commencement and finish of lashings. Pass end A round the stick and cross over B. Pass round stick again and put the end A through the second bight.

(6) *Sheepshank*. Is used for shortening ropes without cutting them. Double the desired length for shortening, then with each standing part make a half hitch round the nearest end of the doubled cord.

(7) *Timber Hitch*. For hauling timber. Take the end of a rope round the timber, then pass round the standing part B and several times round its own part C.

(8) *Fisherman's Bend*. Used for tying two wet ropes. At the end of one rope A make a loose half hitch. Pass the end of rope B through the loose half hitch in an opposite direction to the other rope A. With the end B make a half hitch on A and pull tight.

Section 9

FIRST AID

The following notes are suggestions for dealing with various emergencies likely to befall walkers and campers, and no attempt has been made to give the full treatment. Remember that too much amateur attention in serious accidents may lead to complications. In such cases first aid implies only the necessary treatment to relieve suffering, or prevention of further injury until the arrival of a doctor.

Space will not permit instruction in bandaging, but readers requiring information should consult the bibliography.

Bleeding from the Nose

Not dangerous unless excessive. Lie patient down quietly, and bathe the back of the neck, face and forehead with cold water. If this is not practicable, place handkerchiefs soaked in cold water over the bridge of the nose and back of the neck. Breathe through the mouth while bleeding is in progress, avoid exertion for some time afterwards, and on no account blow the nose.

Bleeding from Cuts and Injuries

If the cut is small, apply tincture of iodine or Friar's Balsam, and if necessary cover with an antiseptic dressing and firm bandage. In more serious injuries an artery may be cut. This will be indicated by the flow being bright scarlet and spurting out in jerks, corresponding with the beat of the heart. Send for a doctor, and without waste of time press on the spot with a linen pad. A handkerchief rolled into a ball and bound firmly will serve in such an emergency. If the bleeding still continues, tie a bandage over the pad, insert a small stick in the knot, and twist until just tight enough to stop the bleeding. Do not retain this tourniquet, as it is called, longer than necessary, as serious harm may be done if the circulation is stopped too long. On the other hand, if a vein is cut, the blood will be dark coloured and flow steadily. The treatment is the same as for arterial bleeding except that much lighter pressure will suffice. In the case of a bleeding varicose vein, lie the patient down, raise the limb, and apply light pressure to the bleeding point. Most people feel faint after the loss of blood, and a cup of hot tea or coffee is advised.

Blisters

See p. 2.

Bruises

Treat first with cold applications. Later a dressing of tincture of arnica or lead lotion will be found useful.

Burns and Scalds

Most painful. Dangers are shock and entry of germs through the injured parts. May be caused by:

Dry heat   .. Fire, hot metal or high-voltage electric current.
Moist heat   .. Scalds.
Friction ..   .. Revolving wheel.
Corrosive acids .. Spirit of salts, sulphuric acid, etc.
Alkalis   ..   .. Caustic soda, ammonia, etc.

In all cases except acids and alkalis the treatment is on the same lines. For a minor burn, where the skin is unbroken, apply a little olive oil, tannic acid dressing, or, if these are not available, a cold-water bandage. Bigger burns must be treated with caution, and require medical attention. Remove clothing round burnt part, and if skin is unbroken apply tannic acid dressing, or, if this is not at hand, strips of lint or handkerchief soaked in a weak solution of baking soda. As a last resort, use strips soaked in warm water. Strips are recommended as they are easier to remove. DO NOT APPLY OIL IN THIS TYPE OF CASE, and on no account remove any clothing which is sticking to the burn. Much relief can be obtained by placing the injured part in water of the same temperature as the body, 98° F., until suitable dressings can be obtained. If the face is burnt, the dressing should take the form of a mask of linen, with holes cut for the eyes, nose and mouth. If the skin is broken, dress with strips of linen soaked in warm water, or preferably a warm solution of bicarbonate of soda. Do not prick blisters, and obtain a doctor in all

4

serious cases. Scalds are treated in the same way as burns. In the case of scalding fat, a handful of flour thrown over the part affected immediately will sometimes absorb the fat and save trouble. Shock may accompany a severe burn or scald. Lay the patient down and apply warmth to the extremities. Loosen any tight clothing and give a hot drink of milk, tea or coffee. Burns by acid—bathe with a weak solution of alkaline lotion such as washing soda, or baking powder, or lime. Burns by alkali—apply a weak acid solution such as lemon juice or vinegar.

Chilblains

Caused by bad circulation or continued exposure to cold and damp. If unbroken, much relief can be obtained by rubbing with the hand or dry friction with a flesh glove. This improves the circulation. A preparation known as Iodex can be applied after rubbing. If the skin is broken, boracic ointment or Iodex gives relief.

Choking

Hold head forward and strike smartly on the back. If this fails, put a finger down the throat and hook the obstruction out. This must be done carefully in order to avoid pushing it further down the throat.

Concussion

If insensibility, however brief, follows a blow on the head, it should be regarded as a case of concussion, and a doctor should be called, in case of possible injury to the brain. Beyond keeping the patient quiet, no other treatment is advisable.

Corns

See p. 2.

Cramp

Due to an involuntary contraction of the muscles, and may be caused by cold or over exertion. The patient should lie down and relax, while the affected part is rubbed vigorously with warm hands.

Drowning

A method of resuscitation when breathing has apparently ceased.

To promote artificial breathing, observe the following instructions:

After a person has been lifted out of the water, and breathing has ceased, immediately turn him face downwards, resting the face on the left cheek, placing the arms at right angles to the body, with the forearm parallel to the body and the hands palm downwards. Remove any obstruction from the mouth and air passages, then kneel at the side of the patient, place your hands in the small of the back, thumbs together and pointing towards the head, fingers closed and slightly pressing into the sides of the body, the little fingers over the lowest ribs. Bend your body slowly forward from the knees, keeping the arms straight, so that all pressure is imparted by the weight of your body. Next swing your body slowly backwards, thus removing the weight from the hands. The forward movement should take two seconds and the backward movement three seconds. Continue to make the combined movements twelve times a minute.

After natural breathing has been established, observe the following instructions:

To promote circulation. Rub the inside of the limbs towards the heart with a firm pressure of the hands. Dry the hands and feet, and as soon as dry clothing can be procured, strip the patient and reclothe or cover with blankets. Continue friction over the dry clothing or under the blankets. As soon as respiration has been completely restored remove patient to a house. Promote warmth by application of hot flannels to the pit of the stomach and hot-water bottles or hot bricks wrapped in flannel to the feet, to the arm-pits and thighs. If the power of swallowing has returned, small quantities of warm water, warm brandy and water, or coffee should occasionally be administered; the patient kept in bed and sleep encouraged. In all cases send for a medical man as soon as possible.

The above is known as the "Schafer" method, and is reprinted by permission of the Royal Life Saving Society. Further details will be found in their instructional handbook.

Eyes

In the case of a foreign body in the eye, do not rub, but try blowing the nose hard—this will often remove dust and small pieces of grit. If unsuccessful, removal can be attempted with the twisted corner of a soft handkerchief. If beneath the upper lid, pull down over the lower lid, to permit the hair of the lower lid to brush the upper. If grit is actually embedded in the eyeball, do not attempt to remove it, but drop in a little castor oil, apply a handkerchief or pad, and seek a doctor's help. Eyes are very delicate, and in any difficulty get a doctor rather than risk the well-intentioned efforts of an amateur.

Earache

Apply warmth, and if pain is severe take a couple of aspirin tablets. Syringing and the use of olive oil require caution and should only be done under doctor's instructions; in fact, any case of earache should be seen by a doctor as soon as possible.

Fainting

If still conscious, sit patient down and bend body forward until the head is between the knees. If unconscious, lay patient down with the head slightly lower than the feet. Loosen all tight clothing and allow plenty of fresh air to circulate round him. When recovered, give warm tea or coffee.

Fracture

A simple fracture is when a bone is broken with no other injury to the surrounding parts. A compound fracture, on the other hand, implies injury to the surrounding parts in addition to the broken bone. Indications of a fracture are:

(a) Considerable pain.

(b) Unnatural position or unnatural movement of the limb.

(c) Crepitation or grating between the broken ends of the bone.

A dislocated limb tends to be rigid and moves in one piece, but a fractured limb, on the other hand, will nearly always move as if it consists of more than one piece. Fractures are obviously the doctor's concern, but if it is absolutely necessary to move a sufferer, the limb must be supported by binding firmly to a stick or piece of board padded with a towel or similar soft material. Remember the possibility of further injury occurring by unnecessary movement. If there is a wound over the site of the fracture, apply an antiseptic dressing.

Hay Fever

Large numbers of people suffer agonies from this complaint. Chronic sufferers can be cured by inoculation, but the treatment is a long one. Keep away from hay and long grass, and do not smell flowers. Salt and water as a gargle and nasal douche will be found helpful, and should be used three or four times a day. Sore and inflamed eyes are another symptom, and should be treated with a weak solution of boracic acid. Dissolve one ounce in one-and-a half pints of water, and use cold in an eyeglass night and morning. Dr. Mackenzie's smelling-bottle, obtainable at any chemist's, is helpful.

Poisoning

Mushroom poisoning and the effects of tainted food should be dealt with by giving an emetic of a tablespoonful of salt or a dessertspoonful of mustard in a tumblerful of water. After the patient has been sick, give a raw egg beaten up in milk, or a cup of tea. Always consult a doctor in poisoning cases.

Sprains

Caused by a violent twist or wrench of a joint, as a result of which there is stretching of the ligaments. Sprains occur most frequently in ankle, wrist and knee. Symptoms—considerable pain and swelling round the joint, and inability to bear weight on the limb. Treatment —cold-water bandages at first, afterwards application of lead lotion and complete rest of the injured part. If in any doubt, assume that a fracture is present, and treat accordingly.

Stings

If the insect's sting is left in, it should be extracted. Dab on dilute ammonia or peroxide of hydrogen. If neither of these are to hand, try a piece of wet washing soda or the household blue bag.

Sunstroke

Remove patient to a cool place. Soak a towel or hand-kerchief in cold water to which a little vinegar has been added, and apply to head and chest. In severe cases apply also to spine. A little weak lime juice, or failing this, cold water, may be allowed.

Section 10

THE HIGHWAY CODE

In the past ten years 64,759 people have been killed and 1,874,339 injured as a result of accidents on the road. A large proportion of these were caused through ignorance and could have been averted with proper care and thought for others.

A growing conviction among all sections of the community that drastic action was necessary has been crystallised by the Minister of Transport, Mr. Leslie Hore-Belisha, who decided that the public required educating in correct road usage. In order to do this satisfactorily, he took the bold step, in the face of considerable opposition from interested parties, to standardise the rules of the road and to frame a code of conduct, which would minimise road accidents if properly understood and carried out.

The result was the publication of "The Highway Code," which deals comprehensively with the conduct of all road users—motorists, cyclists and pedestrians. The Highway Code booklet can be purchased for a penny, and if you are not already familiar with its contents, study it at once. Traffic lights, pedestrian crossings and the Road Code have been forged into an instrument of safety for YOU; make the best use of it, remembering Mr. Hore-

Belisha's final paragraph in his Foreword to the Code, in which he says: "Respect for the Code and for the spirit underlying it is so much a moral duty that its practice should become a habit and its breach a reproach."

Before dealing with the rights and duties of specific road users, the Code propounds certain definite propositions, the more important of which are:

That all persons have a right to use the road for the purpose of passage, but accidents are inevitable unless allowance is made for possible error on the part of others.

It enjoins care and courtesy at all times, and gives a warning that alertness and sense of caution may be affected by alcohol or fatigue.

Very properly you are asked to keep your dog under control, and to this might well be added the word "children." Large numbers of accidents have occurred in attempts to avoid children and dogs which have run into the road suddenly without warning. Do please remember this.

Finally, you are asked to learn the traffic signals used by drivers and those regulating traffic. These are given in the Code and cannot be reproduced here for reasons of space. The same applies to the section for motorists, but the more important paragraphs relating to cyclists and pedestrians are given below in full.

To Cyclists

Keep as near to the left as practicable, unless about to overtake or turn to the right. (This rule does not necessarily apply where there are special traffic arrangements, as in one-way streets or roundabouts.)

Always keep a good look out, especially when riding with dropped handlebars.

Remember that the faster you are travelling, the smaller

is the margin of safety should an emergency arise, and the more serious must be the result of an accident.

Always be able to pull up your cycle well within the distance for which you can see the road to be clear, whether by night or by day.

Take special care when it is foggy, when light is bad, or when roads are wet, slippery or otherwise dangerous.

Remember that you cannot be certain of the movements of pedestrians. Be ready for children who may run suddenly on to the road, and for people who may step from a refuge or footpath. Make allowance for the hesitation of the aged and infirm and for the blind.

Give plenty of room to pedestrians.

Be prepared to meet pedestrians and led animals coming towards you on your own side of the road.

Take special care when passing a stationary vehicle or any other form of obstruction which prevents a clear view of pedestrians or oncoming traffic.

When the traffic in front of you is held up, do not encroach on the offside of the road and thereby impede other traffic.

Do not attempt to gain a forward position in a traffic block by riding along the narrow spaces between stationary vehicles.

Ride in single file whenever road or traffic conditions require it, and never more than two abreast. Avoid riding between tram lines whenever possible; there is a danger that your wheels may skid when passing over the tram lines or catch in the central slot.

Keep a straight course and do not wobble about the road.

Never ride close behind fast-moving vehicles; always leave enough space to allow for their slowing down or stopping suddenly.

Never hold on to another vehicle.

Never carry parcels or other articles which may interfere with your control of your cycle or cause damage to others.

Take special care at cross roads, corners and bends.

When turning from one road into another go slow and give way to any pedestrians crossing the roads out of which or into which you are turning.

Proceed with special care when coming from a minor road into a major road, and give way to traffic on the major road. Unless you have a clear view of the major road in both directions, stop just before entering the carriageway of the major road.

Overtake only on the right, except when a driver in front has signalled his intention to turn to the right. (This rule does not necessarily apply in one-way streets.)

Subject to any local provisions to the contrary, tramcars may be overtaken on either side. Before overtaking a tramcar which is about to stop or is stationary, watch carefully to see if passengers are about to board or alight. Go slow or stop as the circumstances require.

Never attempt to overtake if by so doing you are likely to inconvenience or endanger any other road user.

Avoid overtaking at a pedestrian crossing.

Overtake only if you can do so without forcing the person overtaken or approaching traffic to swerve or slacken speed.

Never cut out, that is, never turn out from the near side of the road sharply without giving ample warning and being satisfied that it is safe to do so.

Never overtake at a blind corner or bend, or at or approaching the brow of a steep hill or a hump-backed bridge.

Never overtake at cross roads.

Keep a good look out for all traffic signals, signs and lines.

Before you stop, or slow down or change direction, give the appropriate signal clearly and in good time.

When approaching a police constable or other person regulating traffic, and where necessary for his guidance, signal the direction in which you intend to go. Do not rely on signals to proceed given by unauthorised persons.

When you are held up at a road junction by a person regulating traffic, do not turn to the left—that is, filter—unless you are given a definite indication to do so by him. (In some districts there may be an exception to this rule at intersections where traffic is controlled by the police and the carriageway is specially marked to indicate that filtration is permitted.)

Look out for pedestrian crossings and make yourself familiar with the rules relating to them.

Give regular attention to your brakes and see that they are always efficient.

Always maintain your tyres in a safe condition.

To Pedestrians

Never walk along the carriageway where there is a pavement or suitable footpath. If there is no footpath, it is generally better to walk on the right of the carriageway so as to face oncoming traffic.

On a pavement or footpath do not walk alongside the kerb in the same direction as the nearer stream of traffic.

Never start to cross the road without first looking right, then left, and keep a careful look out until you are safely across. Be specially careful when the road is slippery and where one-way traffic is in force.

Cross the road at right angles whenever possible.

Take special care if you have to step out from behind

or in front of a vehicle or any other form of obstruction which prevents a clear view of the road.

Where there is a pedestrian crossing, subway, or refuge, make use of it.

Remember that moving vehicles require time to slow down or stop, particularly when the road is wet or slippery.

Unless there are "Cross Now" signals, do not rely solely on light signals when you are crossing the road. Pay attention to the movements of traffic, and particularly of turning traffic.

Never step off a footpath on to the road even momentarily without making sure that it is safe to do so.

At controlled crossings, *i.e.* wherever traffic is controlled by police or signals, cross the road only when the appropriate line of traffic is held up.

Never attempt to cross the road just as the traffic is about to start.

Never stand in the road at blind corners or other places where you may not be seen by approaching drivers or where you may obscure their line of vision.

Light Signals

It is important that all road users should be familiar with the significance of light signals. These apply to all vehicular traffic, including cyclists, and it is an offence under Section 49 of the Road Traffic Act, 1930, to disobey them or any other traffic sign.

RED   means STOP and wait behind the stop
                       line on the carriageway.

RED AND AMBER   means STOP but be prepared to go
                       when the green shows.

GREEN	means PROCEED if the road is clear but with particular care if the intention is to turn right or left.
AMBER	means STOP at the stop line unless the amber signal appears when you have already passed the stop line or are so close to it that to pull up might cause an accident.
A GREEN ARROW	shown with the red signal allows vehicles to proceed in the direction indicated by the arrow.

To Pedestrians

DON'T CROSS	means that pedestrians should not cross the carriageway.
CROSS NOW	is a definite invitation to pedestrians to cross the carriageway.

Pedestrian Crossings

It is an offence under the Pedestrian Crossing Places Regulations to disobey the following requirements:

Drivers of vehicles and cyclists

When you are approaching a pedestrian crossing, proceed at a speed which will enable you to stop before reaching the crossing unless you can see that there is no pedestrian on the crossing.

Where a pedestrian crossing is controlled by police or light signals, allow free passage to any pedestrian who has started to cross before you receive the signal to proceed.

Where a pedestrian crossing is not controlled by police or light signals, give way to any pedestrian on the crossing.

Never stop on any pedestrian crossing unless you are forced to do so by circumstances beyond your control or to avoid an accident.

Pedestrians

A pedestrian may not remain on a pedestrian crossing longer than is necessary for the purpose of passing from one side of the road to the other with reasonable despatch.

The preceding extracts from the Highway Code relating to cyclists, pedestrians, traffic lights and pedestrian crossings are reproduced by kind permission of the Controller, H.M. Stationery Office.

Section 11

RAMBLERS AND THE LAW

The average rambler is not likely to transgress the law even unwittingly, but there are one or two points which if made clear might save delay and inconvenience.

The question of trespass is likely to be of some importance, and is one on which a good deal of misunderstanding exists. The first point to remember is that a trespass is constituted not only by a wrongful entry upon land, but by any unjustifiable interference with the enjoyment of land. You will see therefore that, quite apart from putting your foot on another man's land, you may commit trespass by shooting over it, throwing stones on it, throwing rubbish on it, and the leaning of a ladder against another person's house, even if the end of the ladder is on your own or public property, constitutes a trespass.

There is of course a long way between such acts and any legal consequences, but it is well to bear them in mind, and arising on this it is interesting to remember that it is quite immaterial in law whether the guilty party knows that he was trespassing or not. In actual practice very few people would be so unreasonable as not to accept an apology for a genuine mistake, but, legally, ignorance could not be urged in defence.

It is a very common mistake to assume that damage must be done before a trespasser can be sued, and I have seen some trespassers unnecessarily rude and difficult on the assumption that they were safe legally. This is not the case—immediately you put your foot on another person's property you have technically committed a trespass, and it will not be necessary for the owner to prove damage. Of course, it may well be that the damages awarded by a County Court would be small, but the Judge can also order the defendant to pay all costs.

If accosted and told you are trespassing, explain that it was done in error, apologise politely and withdraw. Do not offer the owner or keeper money or refuse to go, because if a trespasser will not leave land on request, he may be removed, no more force being used than is necessary for the purpose.

Thousands of boards are exhibited on which the threat is made "Trespassers will be prosecuted," and a general idea seems to exist that the threat is an idle one and cannot be put into force legally. This is only a half truth, and legal consequences can follow. The actual position is that although the notices strictly interpreted imply that the police will take action, trespass without malicious damage or theft is not a police offence, and they will not take action. The owner, however, can sue for damages in the County Court, as explained previously.

A landowner is not permitted to set traps to keep off trespassers, and any such action would render him liable to a fine; but he is permitted to set traps and guns on his land for the destruction of vermin. In certain circumstances he might be permitted to protect his dwelling-house by traps, but only between sunset and sunrise. However, you are not likely to wander in the vicinity of private houses after dark, and so the point is merely one of interest.

In considering the question of damage, do not break through hedges, walk through or sit on standing grass destined for hay. Do not lop trees, disturb livestock, smoke in the vicinity of ricks, or throw cigarette ends down in dry grass or hedges. Damage assessed for any of these contingencies might be considerable.

On the other hand, ramblers have the right to use public footpaths, even if they run through private property, as they frequently do. These footpaths are usually shown on the map, but if in doubt you may feel fairly certain that stiles, footbridges, steps and fords denote a public right of way.

A person patrolling with a savage animal is liable for any damage done to people on a public footpath. If, however, you enter a field where no right of way exists and are mauled by an animal actually at large, you must take the consequences as a trespasser.

The setting of snares and traps is prohibited by law, which assumes that any person found taking an animal or bird from a trap is deemed to have set that trap. Should you come across a snare with a rabbit or a hare, leave it alone. If the creature is not dead, and you feel you must interfere for humane reasons, give it a sharp crack on the back of the head with a stick and put it out of pain, but leave it afterwards in the snare as you found it.

The picking of mushrooms on another person's property is not in itself illegal, subject of course to the law of trespass. If, however, the owner plants spawn in his fields, however little, and exhibits a notice intimating that mushroom cultivation is in progress, you may not take them in any circumstances.

Many wild birds have legal protection, but it is not proposed to enlarge on the matter here, as the reader will be a bird lover, or at least one who will not disturb wild life unnecessarily.

The road rights of the rambler are dealt with in the section on the Highway Code, to which reference should be made.

Section 12

AN APPEAL—KEEP ENGLAND BEAUTIFUL

For centuries the unsurpassed scenery of these islands was unspoiled by man. His dwellings, both great and small, his churches, and even his bridges, were born of the soil on which they stood, and merged themselves into the natural beauty of their surroundings, becoming as it were imbued with the soul of the countryside. It must be admitted that this blending was accidental and not by design, as building materials were those obtained near at hand, and the work by local men represented the individuality of their district.

The Industrial Revolution at the beginning of last century marked the commencement of a great change. Rural dwellers were attracted to the towns, and in consequence vast numbers of small ill-conceived houses were raised around the factories. Craftsmanship and design were sacrificed together with health and fresh air to the god "Industrialism," whose creed ignored beauty and tradition, and knew only "profits."

The dawn of the twentieth century and the break up

5

of many large estates marked an appreciable increase in the policy of destruction. This has been gathering impetus as the years pass, until we have now reached a stage when nothing is sacred in the interest of so-called "progress." Not only are countless historic houses and buildings disappearing, but some of our most exquisite scenery is being ruined by unsightly new buildings.

Picturesque country lanes are being thoughtlessly widened for the benefit of those who pass through in cars. Great motor roads cut across the country, bordered by the ribbon building of indescribably ugly houses, which are constructed very often by land speculators whose imagination goes no further than rough-cast bungalows with bath, hot and cold.

Advertisement boards are more profitable than crops; owners of petrol-filling stations apparently feel that sales are increased by the prodigal use of corrugated iron and impossible colour schemes, while whole districts are being devastated by the timber merchants. We ourselves are not free from blame in the unnecessary scattering of litter.

In all this picture of destruction there is, however, some hope. Public opinion is beginning to realise the danger, and in many quarters determined attempts are being made to save what is left from disfigurement and injury. Ponder over the question, and realise what it means. You have inherited much that is beautiful, and must play your part in preserving it for the generations to come.

You can join the struggle immediately in several ways. The litter problem is largely a personal one, and is really a question of tidiness. Why leave your picnic rubbish about? You would not leave paper, tins, banana skins and cigarette packets in your own garden; why leave them on the common or by the roadside? Make a point of burning, burying or taking home all litter. It means so little in the case of one party, but in the aggregate it creates a festering sore on the countryside. Rubbish receptacles are becoming more general. Where they exist, use them, and do not hesitate to point them out politely to any one who is not sufficiently public spirited to do the same.

Village rubbish dumps are sometimes a great eyesore. Accumulations of empty tins, old saucepans, broken china and glass, with here and there a bedstead half buried in rags and paper, harbour rats and form a breeding ground for flies. If you are troubled over such a state of affairs in your own neighbourhood, send for the literature of the Scapa Society, 71, Eccleston Square, London, S.W.1.

Bluebell time always provides some sad spectacles of desecration. The profusion of flowers is a temptation to some to pick more than they can carry conveniently, and in consequence from time to time one sees bundles left to languish and die by the roadside. Exercise restraint in the picking of wild flowers, and in any case do not dig them up by the roots. Primroses, ferns and many similar treasures have disappeared entirely from some localities owing to their wholesale removal by enthusiastic gardeners. Remember every flower allowed to seed may help to increase its kind and give pleasure to others. Do please hesitate, and if you must pick flowers, be reasonable.

Do not walk through or picnic on standing grass. Many a good piece of hay has been destroyed by inconsiderate people flattening the long grass.

Take the greatest care to preserve the countryside from the terrors and wastage of fire. Every year hundreds of acres of heath are blackened by this scourge. Be sure that your picnic or camp fire is built in a safe place, and properly extinguished when no longer required. See that cigarette ends and lighted matches are not thrown down on dry, inflammable material.

In rural areas crude advertisements, very often on hoardings of considerable size, are a source of worry to all who value the amenities of the country. Equally inexcusable are bright-coloured metal plates fixed to the walls of shops and farm buildings. There is no reason why a company, whose premises are situated in another part of England, should, in the course of an advertising campaign, ruin your country lanes and streamsides. If the public refused to buy such goods, these vandals would soon understand that the game was not worth while.

Railway stations are in general great offenders. They seem to have a special aptitude for collecting the unsightly metal plate advertisements, and their general design is inconceivably ugly. There is no necessity for this, as some stations and the advertising methods on the Underground Railway will show.

The passing of the Advertisement Regulations Acts has given local authorities power to frame by-laws to deal with this form of nuisance, but many hesitate to carry out their obvious duty, or do so in a half-hearted manner.

Petrol-filling stations are frequently a serious cause of offence to the amenities of their neighbourhood. The Advertisements Acts do not apply to them, but Section II of the Petroleum (Consolidation) Act, 1928, gave local authorities power to make by-laws to regulate the appearance of petrol stations and to prohibit them altogether in certain circumstances. Here again the results vary with the energy and efficiency of the local Council. If you are a motorist, remember to fill only at stations which are well designed and inoffensive in colour scheme.

Unfortunately commercial interests are not the only concerns which spoil the landscape. Telegraph poles and overhead electricity wires, with or without pylons, represent officialdom's effort to modernise it.

We may blame the speculator who has sold the owner one of those wretched dwellings which will fall down at no distant date, or we may blame the owner, but the real remedy lies in educating ourselves and others to recognise that a house may be equally comfortable and no more costly if built in a subdued design and colour in keeping with its surroundings.

If you want to know more of these problems, write to the Council for the Preservation of Rural England, 4, Hobart Place, London, S.W.1.

Any notes on the preservation of the treasures of the countryside would be incomplete without a reference to the National Trust, which was founded in 1895 for the purpose of preserving lands of beauty and buildings of historic interest for the nation. Ramblers owe a debt to the Trust for preserving and giving them access to thousands of acres which would otherwise be spoiled or lost to the public.

Chapter II

THE FARM

Section 13

FIELD CROPS

Your main interest will probably be in the grain crops, particularly at harvest time from August onward, when the country has mellowed from fresh green into golden yellow. This is the culmination of the farmer's year, and a time of general thanksgiving for the fruitfulness of Mother Earth. To game, however, the cutting of the corn and the resulting bare stubble fields must leave no such feeling, but rather a foreboding of bad times ahead, because these are signs that the shooting season is commencing.

Farming is a business, and everything in the countryside belongs to somebody and is there for a purpose. Gates, for instance, are not put up for seats, and are soon ruined by sitting on them. That dry hurdle is used to stop a gap in the hedge, and is not fuel for a picnic fire. No charge is made for enjoying the beauty of the country, and the pleasure of a ramble can be greatly increased by the friendliness of the farmer. This can only be obtained by respecting his property.

Wheat. Wheat is one of the most valuable of all crops, as we depend upon it for our supply of bread. Immense quantities are imported annually from overseas, as the home-grown supply is insufficient for the needs of the ever-increasing population of these Islands.

Wheat is usually sown in the autumn in soil which has

been ploughed and allowed to remain fallow or unused for a time. It is remarkably hardy as a young plant, and survives the most severe winters, but grows more delicate as it reaches maturity, and indifferent weather between the formation of the ear and ripening may completely ruin a crop.

In its early growth the young wheat resembles grass, but it finally reaches a height of three or four feet, with spikes of three or four inches on top of the stems. These spikes, or heads, are composed of a large number of pointed husks containing the grain massed closely together.

Although it grows in temperate zones all over the world, the vast fields of ripening corn are typical of the English countryside at its best. Wheat is cut by the reaper and binder, and then placed in stooks, which are the familiar groups of standing sheaves seen in the harvest field. This operation is important, in order that the grain may be kept dry, and its value and that of the straw largely depends on the way it is carried out. After drying for a few days, the sheaves are stacked until required for threshing. The best wheat is produced if threshed immediately after cutting, and in addition this prevents wastage and damage from rats. The heavy harvest work usually prevents this being done, and it is stacked until more time is available for the operation.

Barley. Barley is usually sown in March and April, and some varieties mature and ripen in thirteen to sixteen weeks after sowing. The colour of the growing plant is a delicate bright green. It attains a height of about three feet, and the ear is about three inches in length. It may be recognised by the regular arrangement of the closely packed seed husks at the top of the stem, each husk

WHEAT

BARLEY

OATS

having a long whisker giving it an entirely different appearance to wheat. When ripened, the stem is of a glistening yellow colour, and the heads droop. Barley is used for malting and distilling, and for domestic purposes; at least 50 per cent. of the home-produced grain goes for feeding stock.

Oats. A favourite crop in all stock-rearing districts, as the straw is nutritious and much appreciated by stock. The plant is easily affected by frost, and is not sown as a rule until March or April. It is quite distinct from other crops, as the seeds do not grow clustered together in heads, but hang down on small branchlets from the stem in groups of three or four. They are light, and move in the slightest breeze.

Hay. Hay is grass cut and dried in the sun, and is used as fodder for cattle. The name should properly only be applied to the finished product, but is used also for the standing crop.

Haymaking as practised to-day was unknown in ancient times. Before its introduction here a large number of animals were slaughtered in the winter and salted down (beef and mutton), and the others were turned loose to exist on what they could find. The introduction of haymaking gave unlimited scope for the production of winter food, and it is now one of our most important crops.

There are three definite stages—mowing, drying, carrying. Theoretically the best time to cut hay is when the majority of grasses are in full flower. Considerations of weather are of even more importance, as rain can spoil hay completely. June is the usual month to cut, but if the weather is bad, the mowing may be delayed until late August. If this is done, however, most of the grass will have gone to seed and lost its nutritional value. This being the case, you will see haymaking commence about the second week in June. The mowing is performed by the haymower described elsewhere, and after being cut the grass is left to dry and perhaps turned by the pitchfork to assist the process. It is then gathered by the horse hay rake about the third day into windrows, or long parallel lines, from which it is easily loaded by fork on to the cart to be carried to the stack. Very often you will see long endless chains revolving on a frame between two side boards leaning on the rick. This is the elevator, which is used to carry hay to the top of the stack, and is a mighty time-saver.

Do you know how a haystack is constructed? First a layer of branches and straw is placed on the ground to keep the air circulating under the rick. Building commences from the corners, and great care is taken to keep them from slipping. The sides are watched continually to prevent them bulging and catching the wet from the eaves. Finally; when the required height is reached, the stack is built a trifle wider to allow for dripping. The middle is then well filled, trodden down, and rounded to prevent rain coming in. Notice that when the roof is finally made it is steep. You may think this ends the preparation, but it is not the case, as the most important stage is to commence, *i.e.* the natural heating. When used, blocks of hay are usually cut out with the knife, and are about fifty-six pounds in weight. Thirty-six of these constitute a load of eighteen hundredweight.

It is worthy of note that grass is one of the most important crops in British farming, and therefore should be shown the same respect as grain.

Section 14

AGRICULTURAL IMPLEMENTS

You will possibly pass a large number of agricultural implements on your walks, some at work and some at rest, and if you do not know already, it may be of interest to learn their names and uses. Remember, however, that a great many different patterns exist of the same implement, and that agriculture is undergoing a period of transition, which means the gradual disappearance of many horse-drawn implements and their replacement by the tractor.

The Haymower. Up to a few years ago hay was made by laborious cutting with the scythe and gathered together

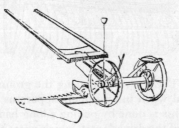

by use of the handrake and pitchfork. The introduction of the horse-drawn haymower has, however, speeded up the process of cutting. This is composed of a seat for the driver, mounted on two wheels, with the cutting instrument, which may be of varying length, fixed on the metal framework at ground-level in front of the wheels. This cutter is composed of a number of slots at the back of which is disclosed the cutting knife. The actual operation consists of the horse or horses drawing the machine along, which causes the grass to be caught up by the slots at ground-level and cut by the knife. The machine is usually horse drawn, but those drawn by motor tractor are increasing. In either case you will have no difficulty in recognising it by the big serrated cutter.

The Horse Rake. Another great time-saver, which obviates the necessity for much individual handraking. It consists of a light iron frame mounted on two fairly big iron wheels, which may be anything from seven to fifteen feet apart. On the back of the machine a hinged iron bar is carried from which long curved steel teeth

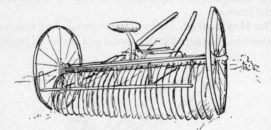

hang over. These teeth slip along the ground gathering the hay, and when full a tipping apparatus empties the machine. This is done by pulling a long handle situated by the side of the driver's seat, which raises the teeth and deposits the load. If you watch one of these machines at work you will notice the tipping occurs at the same positions in each journey up and down the field, which has the effect of depositing the hay in long parallel lines called "windrows." The width of the rake depends to some extent on the length of the cutter, as it is usually twice the length of the cutting blade.

The Hay Sweep. You may often find another imple-ment in use in the hayfield. This consists of a wide wheeled frame on which are fixed iron-pointed wooden poles or teeth, which slide along the ground when in use. Two horses are required, one on each side of the machine, which can collect a cartload of hay with amazing speed, particularly if used on windrows. Another form in use is the tractor-pushed sweep. The use of the sweep is somewhat curtailed if the hay has to be taken through a gate, but if the hay is to be stacked in the same field as it was cut, the advantages of the sweep are obvious.

The Plough. The gardener turns over the upper soil by using the spade, and by exposing the turned earth to the weather, breaks it up and improves crops. This operation is obviously not possible on a large scale in the fields, and so that most useful of all agricultural implements, the

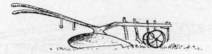

plough, is used. The plough was known in a primitive form in very early times, and while the present-day implement is improved in detail, it relies on the same principles as used by the Egyptians centuries ago. The main idea of the plough is to cut and turn over the surface soil and expose it to the disintegrating effects of sun, rain and frost, which break it up and render it more productive. In its simplest form the implement consists of a slightly curved iron frame, called the beam, dividing out at one end into handles. On the other end two wheels of unequal size are placed, and these determine the width and depth of the furrow, which is the little trench separating two rows of upturned soil. The knife, or coulter, as it is called, is fixed on the bottom of the beam and is capable of adjustment; it is this knife which breaks into the ground and turns over the soil. There are many patterns of ploughs and coulters, and they vary according to the district, the work to be performed, or even the individual taste of the farmer concerned. You will, however, have no difficulty in identifying the implement. Horses have pulled ploughs for centuries, but mechanical power is robbing them of their work, and the motor tractor may now be seen pulling the plough in a very large number of cases.

The Harrow. Is used for levelling the ridges left by the plough, preparing a smooth surface for the seeds, covering the seeds after sowing, or breaking up the top soil.

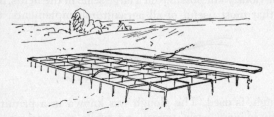

The harrow is as ancient in use as the plough, and in its early days consisted of entwined branches of trees. The type used in the Middle Ages consisted of a wooden frame in which iron pegs, known as tines, were set. The present-day horse-harrow is composed of iron bars in which the tines are set in such a manner that each follows its own track. It is made in two or three sections, which, by folding over one another, give great flexibility on uneven ground, in addition to making the tool more portable. Another type is the chain harrow, which consists of a number of square-cut connected links, which are kept expanded by stretchers and weights. It is used for spreading manure over grassland, levelling and similar purposes. Various other forms exist, the most interesting of which is the disc harrow. This consists of the usual iron frame and driver's seat, but at the back are a number of steel discs about eighteen inches in diameter, which revolve and break up the soil. This type is tractor-drawn.

The Cultivator. Is used for breaking up land. Like the majority of agricultural implements it has an iron frame, supported by two fairly large wheels, on which is a seat for the driver. It has a number of long bent teeth, which can be raised or lowered by the action of a lever at the side

of the driver. It differs from the harrow by the use of wheels and stronger teeth, which may be sharp or blunt, according to the work to be performed. These cultivators vary in type and size down to the small one-horse tool with one or two teeth, and used for close cultivation of crops planted in rows.

The Sower. The old method of scattering seeds by hand has been replaced by mechanical means. There are two methods. In the first, by drill, the seed runs down pipes, and is thus sown in parallel rows. In the second the seed falls on to a piece of close-mesh wire netting, and is thus sown broadcast. In its usual form the implement consists of a long box carried between two high wheels. This box is divided internally into two sections, one of which holds the seed, which drops through holes the size of which can be regulated. In the other section of the box is a long spindle, geared to the ground wheels and carrying small cups. As the driller moves, these cups revolve, scoop up seed and discharge it down little tubes, from which it drops into shallow furrows made by small knives fixed in front of the seed exits. The machine is

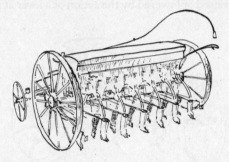

horse drawn as a rule, and from the back has the appearance of a long box from which a number of tubes hang down towards the ground.

The Reaper and Binder. From earliest times the ripe grain has been cut by means of a sickle and bound by hand. The introduction of mechanical means of doing this has, however, revolutionised agriculture and reduced the cost of production. The machine is complicated, but unmistakable by reason of the curious apparatus at the side. This is composed of a number of light wooden frames fixed to a central spindle, which revolves as the machine goes forward, and pushes the standing grain against the platform below, where it is cut by the knives in front. These knives are similar to the haymower, and after the grain has been cut it is tied together by the binding appliance and deposited on the ground—the whole operation is automatic, being one of cut, bind, throw out bundles.

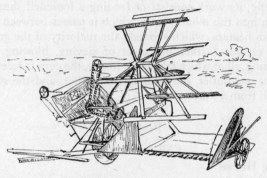

Threshing Machine. Threshing is the process of separating the grain from the husk. In very early times it was probably done by beating out the grain with a stick, but mechanical means have gradually been developed

until the present-day threshing machine has been evolved. It is mounted on four wheels, covered in with a wooden casing, and of considerable size, being drawn, as a rule, by the traction engine which supplies the motive power.

6

It is impossible to get details of such a machine in the space at our disposal, but you will have no difficulty in recognising it when at work in the rickyard or by the rick. The thresher is belt-driven from the traction engine, and, briefly, its work consists of feeding a loosened sheaf of corn into the mouth, from which it passes between two drum beaters, which separate the majority of the grain. By various further processes of sieving, blowing and beating, all of which take place inside, the corn is received from one outlet, the chaff from another, and the straw itself from a third.

Section 15

FARM ANIMALS

The Horse

The horse is of great antiquity, and the fine upstanding specimens of to-day are direct descendants of the small four-toed animals which existed in prehistoric times. It is not known when or where the horse or his distant relative was first subdued and pressed into the service of man, but it was probably somewhere in the East at the dawn of history. Throughout the ages it has always been of first importance, and mention is made of it in the Bible. To-day sees a decline in its use in some aspects of our national life, due of course to the increase in motor-driven vehicles, but the countryman still finds his animals indispensable, and is likely to do so for a long time to come. There are various breeds and varieties, but for our purpose we will examine only the most typical and important.

The Thoroughbred. Is probably the old English horse brought to its present state of perfection by mixing with generations of imported Arab stock. It possesses a beautifully shaped head, tapering and finely set on neck, oblique lengthened shoulders, ample muscular quarters and a long elastic pastern. Quite apart from racing, the thoroughbred is of great value in improving the stock of other breeds. It may be summed up in the words graceful movement, appearance of superb quality even to the untrained eye, and, above all, great speed.

The Hunter. To be ideal should be three-quarters pure bred. He should not be under fifteen hands high, and certainly not over sixteen hands. By the way, to judge the height of a horse requires practice. The unit of measurement is four inches, and is called a hand. If you remember your own height in hands, you will have a good working basis for estimating. Returning to the hunter, you will find him with a smallish head, upstanding in manner, with a broad chest which gives greater room for quickened breathing in the chase. The legs will be shorter than on the thoroughbred, but the action higher. In other words, it is necessary for them to be lifted comfortably and naturally over the many small obstacles found in the field. The general appearance is one of compactness and strength.

The Hackney, or General Purpose Horse. Rarely exceeds fifteen hands in height, and is a hunter in miniature; generally good tempered and safe.

The Suffolk Punch. Is a long low-bodied horse, generally of a chestnut colour, and possessing great power for its weight. It is reputed to give the maximum amount of work on the minimum amount of food, and is a docile, good worker. It is an old breed; said to have descended from the Norman stallions and Suffolk cart mares.

The Shire. Is seventeen hands, and our biggest and strongest horse. Broad of shoulder and of a variety of colours, often of a deep bay with blackish legs, the shire personifies strength and endurance.

The Farm Horse. Is not of any particular breed, colour or size. He is usually of a heavy type; strong and adaptable, as he is used for a variety of purposes.

The Pony. There are many different breeds. They are hardy, strong and can take a greater weight in proportion to their size than any horse.

The Cow

Shorthorns. Are the best general purpose animals, and produce both good meat and milk. About seventy-five per cent. of the pure-bred cattle in this country to-day are shorthorns. They are of a gentle disposition and mature early, gaining enormous weights in a short space of time. Shorthorns have a fine glossy coat of red, red and white, or roan colour, but are not spotted. The nose and skin round the eye are of a rich creamy colour, and the head is small, with short, smooth, white horns. The body is square, and the tail of moderate size.

Jerseys. Are of a rich fawn, or varying shades of golden brown; sometimes inclined to a browny grey, but without white marking. They are slender in body with hips wide apart, and straight legs. Jerseys have a gentle expression, and upward curved black horns; the tongue is also black. They are first-rate dairy cows in every respect.

Guernseys. Are essentially dairy cows. They are similar to Jerseys, but a little less rich in colour and not quite so refined in appearance.

Friesians. The distinguishing colour is black and white, with a square-cut body. Usually owned by specialist breeders and kept in herds.

Kerrys. Black in colour, with long, well-formed, delicately curved horns. Slender in body, with straight backs.

Herefords. Red with white face, chest and under part; the legs are white to the knee, and the tail is of the same colour. It is broad between the eyes, and has a large head carrying medium length horns, which are white with a black tip. The nose is flesh coloured. Herefords are poor milkers, but good for beef.

Red Polls. Not very plentiful except in Norfolk and Suffolk. They are a deep chestnut red, and have a long face with a docile expression. Hornless.

Pigs

The Berkshire. Black with white on the face and tail. Has a short face with a broad snout; is wide between the ears, which are carried erect. The legs are short, straight and strong. The black hair is long, fine and plentiful.

The Large White. Is large but not coarse. It is white in colour, free from black hair and as far as possible blue spots. It is wide between its long thin ears, which are fringed with fine hair. The legs are straight, sitting level with the outside of the body, and the tail is long with a tassel of fine hair at the end. The body is free from wrinkles, and the pig has a gentle disposition.

The Middle White. This is the finest all-round pig known to the breeder, and is kept widely. It is absolutely docile, and similar in all respects to the large white except that it is smaller.

The Large Black. A very popular breed, and kept almost everywhere in England. It is all black, but similar in shape and general characteristics to the large white. Has a fine soft black coat of straight silky hair, which is not too plentiful.

The Tamworth. The only red breed of pigs in this country. It has golden red hair, free from black, and a flesh-coloured skin. The Tamworth is wide between the ears, and has a fairly long straight snout, large ears with a fine fringe.

The Wessex Saddleback. Has a black head and neck with white forelegs and a white saddle over the shoulders. The body, hind legs and tail, which carries a tassel, are black. The snout is fairly long, and the nose is black and velvety in appearance, and you should have no difficulty in identifying the breed. The saddleback is kept in many places as a grazing pig, and is considered excellent as a bacon producer.

Sheep

Sheep have been associated with mankind for centuries, and they fulfil the dual purpose of providing food and clothes. While millions are bred in Australia and South America, the English sheep industry flourishes. The general farmer finds them of great utility, because while they are cheap to feed, they manure the soil for future crops. There are some thirty breeds in Great Britain, but we can only consider one or two of the most typical; in any case, many of them are very similar. They may be divided into three sections: (*a*) the long-woolled breeds, (*b*) the short-woolled breeds, (*c*) the mountain breeds.

LONG-WOOLLED BREEDS

The Lincoln. Is the best-known and most popular long-woolled breed in the world, and is the biggest sheep kept in Great Britain. It has rather a coarse-looking body and long wool, is hornless, and has a white face.

SHORT-WOOLLED BREEDS

The Southdown. Is bred extensively, and is noted for the quality of its mutton. The face is of an even drab colour, without any black or white. In general appearance the animal is well developed, firm and covered with a close even fleece down to the knees.

The Suffolk. Long black face, with moderately long black ears. Hornless. The legs and feet are straight and black. Fleece short.

The Dorset Horn. Is of medium size, and has thin curled horns, a long thin face, with flesh-coloured lips and nose. Compact and of alert appearance. This breed supplies the early market with lamb.

Chapter III

BOTANY

Section 16

COMMON TREES

The Ash. The bark is pale grey covered with a number of irregular dents running upwards. The trunk rises to some height and has curved branches which droop slightly. The tree, which may rise to a height of one hundred feet, is extremely graceful, but has an appearance of strength. The leaflets occur in pairs of four or even six opposite one another on the stalk, with a single terminal leaflet at the top. They are lance-shaped with toothed edges. The roots of the ash extend deeply into the soil, absorbing the nourishment and starving all plants in the vicinity.

The Beech. Lives to a great age and reaches one hundred feet in height. One of the main characteristics of the trunk, particularly in woods where the trees are close together, is the fact that it will often grow perpendicularly to a height of some sixty feet before branching. If the tree is solitary in the open, it will of course grow branches much lower down. The bark is smooth and grey, and as the tree has surface roots, they are often much in evidence, spreading above the soil round the bottom of the trunk. The main branches spread horizontally, but have an upward trend. The leaves are oval, running to a sharp point at the top. In spring they are almost transparent, but later become opaque. At the approach of autumn

ASH

BEECH

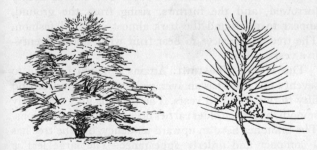

CEDAR OF LEBANON

they change in colour, first to yellow and later to a wonderful golden brown.

The Cedar of Lebanon. Varies greatly in height from fifty to one hundred feet, with a rough brown trunk. Claimed by many to be one of the longest-living trees. At a low level the cedar throws out enormous branches, which grow horizontally, and at this point the trunk divides into a number of spreading branches, giving the general appearance of platforms, surmounted by a flattened crown. The dark-green needle-shaped leaves, rarely more than an inch in length, grow in tufts.

The Deodar is another variety of Cedar, and may be recognised by its accurate growth in the form of a pyramid.

The Sweet Chestnut. A rapid grower in suitable situations, and will attain a height of fifty feet in as many years. If conditions are not particularly favourable, it will throw out enormous branches ten or twenty feet from the ground, and make up in girth what it lacks in height. The sweet chestnut is reputed to be able to outlive the oak, but five hundred years may be taken as the maximum. The elliptical leaves, sometimes ten inches in length, have a fine tooth-like edge. The bark is deeply furrowed, and the furrows, rising from the ground, appear to go round the bark almost in spiral fashion. The tree commences to bear fruit when about twenty-five years old.

The Horse Chestnut. Attains a height of sixty to seventy feet, and has an average life of one hundred and fifty to two hundred years. The trunk is grey and fairly smooth, but when older carries deep twisting undulations The branches have an upward tendency, but the tree has a compact and orderly appearance. The large leaf is composed of five to seven leaflets, each being large,

SWEET CHESTNUT

HORSE CHESTNUT

ELM

narrow at the base opening to an oval top, and often mistaken for a complete leaf.

The Elm. A typical English tree, which reaches a height of one hundred and twenty feet, with a maximum circumference of twenty feet. The life of an elm may be put at not more than three hundred and fifty years. Usually one or two very large branches grow out about midway up the trunk, with perhaps a huge fork at the top, giving the tree an irregular shape and top-heavy appearance. A good deal of young growth can be found low on the trunk. The leaves are oval and run to a well-defined point; the sides are cut into a large number of small teeth. In autumn the foliage turns first an orange colour, then to a very pale yellow, and falls in showers. The elm is a dangerous tree, owing to its habit of suddenly dropping one of its heavy branches, although it appears perfectly sound.

The Silver Fir. Usually grows about one hundred and twenty feet, but there are many cases where a much greater height has been recorded. Its trunk is straight and erect; the bark smooth and greyish brown, but becomes rough with age. Lives three hundred and fifty to four hundred years. The branches grow out at right angles to the trunk, and the tree presents the neat appearance of an elongated cone with a flattened top. The slender flat leaves are arranged along the twigs in dense rows.

The Douglas Fir. Grows rapidly, and in this country reaches one hundred feet. In Canada it may be found twice as high. The trunk bears a thick reddish-brown bark, and the tree is loosely branched in horizontal tiers, giving it a graceful and almost feathery appearance with the top ending almost in a point. The branchlets carry large numbers of slender green leaves of about an inch in length.

SILVER FIR

DOUGLAS FIR

LIME

The Lime. Do not base your idea of the lime tree on the much-pruned specimens seen in towns. If allowed to develop in its natural state it will sometimes rise to ninety feet. The average duration of life may be said to be four hundred years. The trunk is dull grey with long furrows running upwards, and in a confined space it will rise to a considerable height before throwing out branches. If in the open by itself, the lime will, however, branch quite near the ground. The general shape is oval at the top, and thickly branched in the main part. In spring the young leaves are yellowy green. They are heart-shaped, one side being slightly longer than the other, with edges bearing a large number of saw-like teeth. The leafing period is short, as limes are practically the last trees to put out their leaves and the first to lose them. The flowers have a strong sweet smell.

The Oak. Most typical of all British trees. The age of an oak can hardly be measured in terms of human life. The tree does not produce an acorn until it is seventy years old, and should be between one hundred and two hundred years of age before it produces its best timber. It is agreed that quite a considerable number of oaks must have been in existence for more than a thousand years. It has a sturdy twisted trunk of light grey, which in aged trees has tremendous girth. Its height may be anything up to one hundred and twenty feet. In appearance the tree is broad and rounded at the top, with a horizontal line at the bottom caused by the massive lower limbs. The leaves are tough, and divided into about eight rounded divisions.

The Scot's Pine. The typical pine tree of Northern Europe. Is a rapid grower and reaches one hundred feet. The bark is thick, coarsely fissured, and of a browny purple colour. Branches form at intervals, and the

OAK

SCOT'S PINE

PLANE TREE

general appearance is conical with succeeding platforms bending down at the edge. As the tree grows older it sheds its lower limbs, while the upper branches continue to grow, giving the tree a curious flat-topped shape. The bluish green leaves grow from the stem in pairs, and these pairs are massed together in considerable numbers.

The Plane Tree. Has been found particularly suitable for planting in London and is a familiar sight in many streets. It has a tall, straight trunk, which grows up to sixty feet, and in specially favourable circumstances to eighty or ninety feet. It flings out crooked branches some distance from the ground, and is somewhat irregular in outline. The plane has a smooth, grey, thin bark, which is thrown off by the expansion of the softer bark beneath. This is not all cleared at once but falls in big flakes, leaving bright yellow patches and supplying an easy method of identification. It is this throwing off of bark, or spring cleaning, which makes the tree suitable for London. The leaves have three main ribs, and are divided into five indented lobes ending in points. They are bright green in colour, smooth and firm, growing singly and not in pairs. Any accumulation of soot on the leaves is not absorbed but washed away by a shower of rain, leaving them free to breathe again and maintain the health of the tree.

The Lombardy Poplar. Branches grow from ground-level perpendicularly, and give the appearance of a number of small trunks joined together. The leaves are smooth, dark-green, glossy, heart-shaped and finely toothed. The poplar grows rapidly, particularly during the first twenty years, and may reach sixty feet during this period. When fully grown it attains double this height. The tree is spire-shaped, caused by its branches growing upwards fairly closely to the stem.

Another variety is the Old English Black Poplar, which has similar leaves but great straggling branches, which

give it a somewhat untidy outline. The bark is grey, but shows a number of swellings or bumps on the trunk.

The Sycamore. Grows to a height of sixty feet and has a smooth veined bark. It possesses a firm upright trunk, with the lower branches growing out horizontally some distance from the ground, and the upper branches at an angle of forty-five degrees. The leaves are blue-green on the under side, have five lobes like a plane, but grow in pairs. They have toothed edges and the leaf stalk is a reddish colour.

The Walnut. A handsome tree, growing fifty to sixty feet high, which divides into great branches quite low down the trunk; these branches have an upward trend rather than horizontal. The bark is pale grey and much ridged. Average age five hundred years. Carries a mass of long leaves, composed of two or three pairs of lance-shaped leaflets opposite each other with one terminal leaflet. These leaves possess a curious sweet scent, about which varying opinions exist. The walnut does not bear

7

SYCAMORE

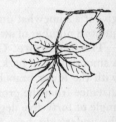

WALNUT

YEW

fruit until twenty years old, and good crops may be anticipated every second season. The unripe fruit can be pickled, but if you collect the ripe nuts from their roughened cover, remember to wear a glove unless you are prepared to have your hands unpleasantly stained.

The Yew. Was used in the Middle Ages to provide bows for the bowmen of England. A slow grower which has the habit of throwing up branches from its base, which join with the trunk, giving it great girth. Possesses a thin reddish-brown bark which peels off easily. The yew does not grow to any great height, but averages from twenty to fifty feet. Great uncertainty exists as to the lifetime of this tree; without doubt it has a long life, but many estimates of some existing trees are probably greatly exaggerated. The branches grow out gracefully, giving it in general a semicircular appearance. The leaves are narrow and pointed, about one inch long, and grow in great numbers set in opposite sides of the twig.

Section 17

FRUITS AND BERRIES

EDIBLE

The Sloe. Grows mainly in the hedgerow on a black-barked shrub which has very sharp spines. The fruit is round, about a quarter of an inch in diameter, and grows in small groups. It is held up by a small stalk, and is black, but the natural colour is hidden by a thick bloom which produces a purplish effect. The sloe has a very harsh taste, which sets the teeth on edge, but when ripe—and you may decide this by the slightly wrinkled skin—its taste is not unpleasant. Gathered in bulk, sloes make a very palatable wine, or the much esteemed sloe gin.

The Bullace. Grows on a brown-barked shrub, which has a few spines. The black or yellow fruit droops from the branches, and is larger than a sloe, often being an inch in diameter. The leaves of the shrub are downy underneath, and offer a clue to identification.

The Wild Plum. The bark is brown, but spineless, and the down on the leaves is restricted to the ribs on the under side only. The fruit, which is black and covered with bloom, grows to one and a half inches in diameter. Found occasionally in the hedgerow, but not so plentiful as sloes and bullaces.

Crab Apples. Very small yellow and red apples, hung by slender stalks. They are about an inch in diameter, very acid in taste, and not really fit for human consumption; some, however, eat and appear to enjoy them. Crab-apple jelly may be made by stewing the fruit whole, pressing it through a fine sieve and afterwards boiling the pulp with sugar.

Blackberries. September sees the blackberry harvest, and the hedges are dotted with red, purple or black, according to the degree of ripeness. The berries are easy to pick when ripe, but more difficult when red and only half ripe. This is clearly a method adopted by the blackberry to propagate itself, because the seeds are distributed by birds eating and dropping them elsewhere. As they will not germinate until ripe, it is therefore necessary for the blackberry to induce the birds to pluck ripe fruit only. The simple expedient of making the ripe fruit easier to pick works perfectly, as you may notice the birds try two or three berries sometimes before they manage to find a ripe one. If you intend to collect the berries yourself, take an open-mouthed stiff basket with a wide handle which can be carried on the arm, and do not forget a hooked stick.

Elderberries. Grow in large groups of small round berries of a purple-black colour, and without much flavour. These berries can be used for making elderberry wine, which is much esteemed in the countryside. The tree grows to a height of about twenty feet, and has leaves divided into seven or more toothed leaflets. Not pleasant to eat, and sometimes disagree with people.

Yew Berries. The yew berries are little red wax-like cups encircling the seed. They are not poisonous providing you do not eat the seed ; but they are not recommended, as they have a sickly taste.

The Medlar. The fruit is somewhat pear-shaped, and of a brown colour. It is not considered suitable for eating until October, by which time the skin has shrivelled and the fruit is soft and almost rotten. Some people consider it very good, but opinions vary. The spiny tree is about twenty feet high.

The Hazel Nut. Found in the hedges and grows in groups. The smooth nuts are clearly seen, but are held in position by a ragged tough husk.

Sweet Chestnuts. The familiar glossy brown nuts are encased in a very thickly spined coat, which splits and discloses two or three chestnuts in October.

Beech Nuts. The beech produces a bristly closed box, which splits open into four wings and reveals the three-sided sharp-edged nuts called "beech mast."

POISONOUS OR NOT RECOMMENDED FOR EATING

Black Bryony. The berries, which are rather larger than red currants, and much the same colour, hang in clusters. The plant takes its name from the purple black leaves, which are heart-shaped and glossy. It climbs about the hedge with long trailing stems. White bryony, on the other hand, has fingered leaves, which are not glossy, and much smaller berries.

Dogwood Berries. Grow in the hedge on a shrub which grows about six feet high. It is easily distinguished, as the oval leaves which are pointed and veined turn purple in autumn. The stalks are also purple. The black berries grow in flat loose clumps and ripen in September.

The Spindle Tree. A slender bush with angular twigs. In autumn the bright red seed-pods open and disclose the orange seeds within. The whole effect is most decorative. The shrub gets its name from the wood being formerly used for making skewers and spindles.

Wild Arum. The orange-scarlet berries stand up on short thick stalks in the hedgebank, where the arum bloomed in the summer. The leafy envelope and leaves are now decayed, and the ground being bare all round makes them very conspicuous.

Holly Berries. Are familiar to all. They ripen in the late autumn but do not appear to be very inviting to birds, as they are usually left until all other supplies have been exhausted. In fact, it is no uncommon sight to see the flowers of one year on the tree at the same time as the berries of the previous crop. Some varieties produce yellow berries, but they are not common.

Hips. The scarlet fruits of the dog rose are a common sight in autumn, and are known as hips.

Haws. The familiar crimson berries of the hawthorn, which are egg-shaped, each hanging loosely on a medium-length stem. They are about a quarter of an inch in diameter, and beneath the flesh there is a hard bony core. In good years these berries are so numerous as to give the tree or hedge a crimson tint when viewed from a short distance. Hips and haws can be eaten, but I cannot recommend them, and personally prefer to leave them for the birds.

The Acorn. The highly polished egg-shaped acorn resting in its rough cup needs no description, but a reminder may be worth while, that it makes better food for pigs than for human beings.

Horse Chestnuts. The rich mahogany-coloured nuts, or conkers, are encased in twos and threes in a thick, round, green covering protected by sharp, stout spikes, set well apart. It should be remembered that these spikes are much bigger and less numerous than those on the sweet chestnut.

Deadly Nightshade. The berries grow singly, about the size of a small cherry, and lie in a spreading green collar. They are usually shiny, purple or black, and are seen on a somewhat untidy green plant about two feet high. Exceedingly poisonous.

Woody Nightshade. The berries are deep purple or black, but much smaller than those of the deadly night-shade, and grow in clusters. An additional mark of dis-tinction is that the woody nightshade is a climber and straggles over the hedgerow.

Section 18

WILD FLOWERS

WHITE FLOWERS

Wood Sorrell. April to September. Moist shady woodlands and hedgerows. Height two to three inches. Clover-shaped leaves, each on a single, round, smooth stem. These leaves are green on top with purple under sides, and droop at night into folds with the green uppermost. The small white flowers with purple veins grow singly, each on its own stem.

Wild Strawberry. April to August. Woods and shady situations. Low and creeping, which form roots. Three egg-shaped hairy leaflets with serrated margins at the end of each stalk. Flowers are white, somewhat resembling a minute buttercup. The small strawberries are an excellent flavour.

Common Daisy. All the year round. Found everywhere. Has rosettes of oval-shaped leaves from among which the flower stalks grow, each bearing a single bloom. The white inflorescence, sometimes tinged with pink, radiates from a yellow centre. The flowers close at night and during wet weather.

Grass of Parnassus. July to October. Bogs and damp places. Height nine inches. Has a rosette of stalked, heart-shaped leaves from which rise long flowering stems. Flowers are creamy white with green veins, saucer-shaped, with five petals.

Shepherd's Purse. All the year round. Fields and roadsides. Height one foot. Hairy stem, with long deeply indented leaves. Minute white flowers without scent. The seed vessels are green and heart-shaped.

Ox-eye Daisy. May to September. Fields and meadows. Height one to two feet. Smooth hard stem with long indented leaves, which narrow towards the base. Flower may be described as a large daisy with a broad white inflorescence and a yellow disc for centre. Known in Scotland as the gowan.

White Deadnettle. All the year round. Roadside, field and pasture land. Height one foot. Hairy square stem. Leaves resemble those of the nettle, but do not sting. They grow in pairs, one each side of the stem, and each pair is at right angles to those immediately below.

The flowers are white and grow in clusters of six or eight at the junction of leaves and stem.

White Bedstraw (also Yellow). June to August. Hedges and fields. Height one to three feet. Stems thin and hairy, round which the leaves grow in rings. Small white flowers form clusters on short stalks up the stem.

Greater Stitchwort. April to July. Meadows, pastures and hedges. Height one to two feet. Stems square, erect and brittle. Not strong and therefore leans against other plants for support. Sharp-pointed long leaves are arranged in pairs. Has white flowers growing on separate stalks. Each flower resembles a ten-pointed star, as the five petals are cleft almost to the base. They measure three-quarters of an inch across.

Water Buttercup, or Water Crowfoot. April to July. Streams and ponds. Stems smooth, round and generally submerged. Leaves of two kinds: those floating on the surface are kidney-shaped and glossy; those under the water consist of threadlike branches. Flowers are white, shading to yellow towards the centre.

Jack-by-the-Hedge, or Hedge Garlic. April to July. Shady hedgerows. Height two to three feet. Stems round and smooth, often bending down rather than erect. Leaves on long stalks are heart-shaped, heavily toothed at edge and hairy beneath. The white blooms, rather like small wallflowers in shape, are arranged along the top of the stem. The seed pods, about two inches long, are narrow and point upwards. The plant has a strong smell of garlic when crushed.

Fool's Parsley. July to September. Hedges and cultivated fields. Height two to four feet. Stems round and hollow. Leaves smooth and fernlike. Flowers grow in small white clusters, which form a big group at the top of the stem. Unpleasant smelling.

Wild Carrot. May to August. Hedges. Height two to four feet. Tough, grooved, rigid stem covered with white hairs. Leaves fernlike, with a hairy under side. Flowers grow in small white clusters, gathered together into a saucer-shaped head.

White Comfrey. May to August. Streamsides and damp ditches. Height two to three feet. Rough hairy stem and long lance-shaped leaves, which increase in size towards the bottom of the stem. The flowers, creamy white or sometimes purple, are bell-shaped and grow in small drooping clusters at the top of the stems.

Meadow Sweet, or Queen of the Meadows. May to August. Streamsides and damp meadows. Height three to four feet. Stems furrowed, woody, and of red tint. Leaves are dark-reddish green, irregularly toothed, with the under surface white and downy. The small creamy white flowers are massed in great clusters at the top of the stem. Pleasant smelling.

Cow Parsnip, or Hogweed. June to September. Meadows and hedgerows. Height four to six feet. Stems are thick, rough grooved, hairy and hollow. Leaves are broad and much indented. Flowers are white, sometimes a pink shade, and form a cluster or head at the top of the stem.

Hemlock. June to August. Hedgerows and waste places. Tall, up to six feet in height. Can be recognised by stem, which is smooth and dotted with dull purple. The leaves are large and divided like those of a fern. The tiny white flowers grow in big flat clusters at the top of the stems. The plant has a mousy smell, and is very poisonous. It is supposed to have supplied the poison from which the Greek philosopher, Socrates, met his end.

Traveller's Joy, called also **Wild Clematis** and **Old Man's Beard.** June to September. Climbs in the hedge, particularly in chalky districts. The tough stem of great length climbs by means of leaf stalks, which twist round any support. It has small clusters of white flowers, which later develop into feathery tufts.

Great Bindweed, or Hedge Convolvulus. July to August. Hedgerows. Delicate long stems, actually climb round the bushes and shrubs on which they live, and do not use tendrils or climbing shoots. The leaves are heart-shaped. Flowers are large white trumpets, which close at night, but remain open in the rain.

Small Bindweed. July to August. Hedgerows and fields. Climbs in the same way as its bigger brother. Leaves are well veined and shaped like an arrow head. Flowers are trumpet-shaped, usually white but sometimes pink, and close in wet weather.

Goosegrass, or Cleavers. May to August. Hedges. Climber with weak, rough, square stems, from which side branches grow in pairs. The leaves, covered with hairy prickles, grow in circles round the stem. The very small white flowers form on long stalks. The small round fruits stick to the clothes and stockings.

Chickweed. All the year round. Found everywhere. A climber with a much-branched stem of considerable length. Leaves are stalkless, oval and in pairs. Very small white flowers grow in clusters at the top of the stems.

White Bryony. May to September. Does not survive the first frost. Woods and hedges. Climber and stems often of great length. Leaves are four to five inches across and covered with rough hairs on each side. They are heart-shaped but indented. The flowers are small, white, green veined and hairy.

White Violet. February to April. Woods and hedge-row banks. Height one to two inches. Leaves heart-shaped. A variety of the ordinary sweet-scented violet, and, like the latter, produces, in addition to its white flowers, small green bud-like growths which never open, but set and produce seed.

White Clover. May to November. Meadow and pasture land. Usually short, but if growing in long grass will attain a considerable length to reach the light. Has long creeping stems which root at the joints. The leaves are trefoil. The flowers are white, tinged with pink, and combine together to form a head, which possesses a pleasant smell.

YELLOW FLOWERS

Coltsfoot. February to May. Fields. Height three to four inches. In very early spring this plant sends up a hollow stalk covered with small pointed woolly scales. From this a single, bright yellow flower head, something like a dandelion, develops. The leaves appear after the flowers, and are broad and heart-shaped with a toothed margin.

Cowslip. May to June. Occasionally in mild weather from March onwards. Meadow land and hedgebanks. Height six to ten inches. Long, round, downy stems standing erect high above the leaves, which resemble those of the primrose, but are somewhat shorter and rounder and grow in rosettes. The flowers are rich deep yellow, carrying one orange spot. They are somewhat like a primrose, but droop and carry several blooms on each stem.

Primrose. March to May. If weather mild, a few venturesome blooms will appear very early in the year. Banks, sheltered hedgerows, and woodlands. Grows low to ground. Leaves are large, dull green, soft and crumpled. Each stem carries one flower of a pale yellow colour, which spreads in a star-like shape from a green cup.

Dandelion. March to October. A few solitary specimens from January onwards. Grows everywhere. Stems are hollow and give out a milky fluid when broken. The leaves grow from the root, are long, indented and narrower towards the base. Flowers are bright yellow, shaped something like a daisy and have a small green centre, generally not visible. Seeds form in feathery balls, to be blown away by the wind.

Groundsel. Flowers all the year round. Occurs everywhere. Height six to ten inches. Sticky, woolly stem. Smooth, much-indented leaves, and small yellow flowerheads, somewhat egg-shaped.

Yellow Rattle. May to July. Pastures and damp places. Height six to eighteen inches. The long narrow leaves and the yellow flowers resemble those of the nettle in shape.

Kidney Vetch, or Lady's Finger. June to August. Dry banks. Height six to twelve inches. Woody stems. Leaves are each composed of a number of long leaflets. Flowers are pale yellow, gathered together in heads; two heads frequently grow together at the top of the branches.

Lesser Celandine. February to May. Sunny banks, pastures. Flower stalks are longer than the leaf stems, which are about six inches in length. The leaves vary, some being heart-shaped, while others at the top of the stem are ivy-shaped. The flowers are bright yellow, many-petalled stars.

Charlock, or Wild Mustard. May to August. Usually grows in masses in fields and meadows. Height one to two feet. Stem erect and hairy. Leaves rough with long-toothed edges. Flowers are bright yellow, having four petals, and form a spike of colour at the end of the stem.

Tormentil. June to August. Moors and meadows.

Height six to twelve inches. Stems rarely erect, silky haired and much branched. Leaves consist of five deeply toothed stalkless leaflets growing from the stem. The small yellow flowers have four petals and resemble a Maltese cross. They grow singly on short stalks, which spring from the leaf joints.

Yellow Goat's Beard. June to August. Pastures. Height eighteen inches. The leaves are long, narrow and sharp pointed. The large yellow flower heads have blunt petals, and the daisy-like blooms are only open in the early morning and close about 11 a.m.

Agrimony. June to September. Wayside and edge of meadows. Height two feet. Erect stem, and leaves consist of seven large serrated hairy leaflets. Small, pale yellow flowers, which grow all the way up the long slender stem.

Yellow Flag. May to July. Marshes and boggy pools. Height two feet. The stem is round and the leaves long and sword-shaped. The large, bright yellow flowers are similar in every way to the common garden iris or flag.

St. John's Wort. July to September. Copses and hedgebanks. Stems are smooth, pale brown and two-edged. The leaves are small, oval and without stems, and have a sweet, aromatic smell when crushed. The yellow flowers have five petals, surrounding a mass of long stamens of the same colour.

Marsh Marigold, or King Cup. February to August. Marshy fields and by ponds and streams. Stems are thick and hollow. The leaves are a glossy deep green above and a lighter colour beneath. They are heart-shaped and increase in size considerably after flowering time. Deep rich golden flowers, like large buttercups.

Meadow Buttercups. June to July. Fields, meadows and pastures. Height one to two feet. Stem ridged and hairy. Leaves fernlike. The flowers consist of five golden petals, with a mass of short upright stamens in the centre.

Sowthistle. May to August. Waysides. Height two to three feet. The stem is thick and branched, and of a glossy, dark green colour. The flowers are something like a small dandelion in shape, and grow from the tops of the branches. When broken, the stem exudes a white milky liquid.

Broom. April to June. Heaths and commons. Height three to six feet. Grows as a bush, without prickles. Leaves are each composed of three leaflets. Flowers are bright yellow, rather larger than those of the furze, and are of a rather peculiar shape. Of the five petals, one is very large and erect; two lateral petals are like wings, uniting with the two bottom ones, which are boat-shaped.

Gorse, Furze, or Whin. All the year round. Heaths and commons. Height three to four feet. Grows as a bush. Leaves are sharp spines, protecting the plant from browsing animals. Flowers are small, yellow, possessing a pleasing coconut-like smell, and grow from the spines.

Ragwort. June to November. Everywhere. Height three to four feet. Stem is coarse looking and ribbed. The leaves are very much indented and present a ragged appearance. Flower heads resemble a daisy with a deep yellow centre and lighter yellow petals radiating from it. They grow on their own stalks, which form large conspicuous heads. The plant gives out an unpleasant odour when bruised.

Great Mullein. June to August. Banks and roadsides. Height two to six feet. The leaves growing near the ground are large, thick, and very woolly in appearance. Stem is stout and erect. Pale yellow flowers grow for a considerable distance down the stem, forming a dense yellow spike.

Silverweed. June to September. Wayside. Creeper. The smooth round stems, creeping along the ground, throw out rootlets at intervals, which propagate new plants. The leaves are green on top but silver in colour underneath. Each flower grows on its own stalk, has five golden petals, and is somewhat like a small wild rose in shape.

Rock Rose. June to September. Chalk downs and banks with gravel soils. The plant is low lying, and the branches trail along the ground. The small oblong leaves are hairy on their upper surface and downy below. The yellow flowers, about an inch in diameter, are like a buttercup, but the petals have the softness of a poppy.

Honeysuckle. May to September. Woods and hedgerows. The tough stems, sometimes twenty feet long, always twine from left to right. The stalkless leaves, green in colour, but sometimes tinged with red, are egg-shaped, and grow in pairs. The flowers, which are of a creamy yellow colour merging into pink, consist of lipped tubes growing in a cluster at the end of the stems. Sweet scented.

BLUE FLOWERS

Bluebell, or Wild Hyacinth. March to May. Woods and open glades. Height six to nine inches. Long, narrow, sword-shaped leaves stand erect. The stems are soft, round and droop slightly when the rich bluebell flowers are out at the top.

Harebell. June to September. Dry meadows and heaths. Height six to twelve inches. Stems are thin but wiry. The first leaves, which grow from the root, are rounded. Later the stem leaves appear, which are like grass. The flowers, usually blue, but sometimes white, hang gracefully like little bells.

Cornflower. July to August. Cornfields. Height two feet. Possesses strong stem. Upper leaves are long and sword-like, but lower leaves are deeply lobed, and both are covered with down. The flower heads grow singly at the top of the stems, and are composed of a brilliant blue outer fringe of sterile flowers encircling a central group of fertile flowers.

Brooklime. July to September. In water or by water side. Height six to nine inches. Stems thick and soft, sending down roots at the joints. The leaves, one on each stalk, are pale green, rounded and egg-shaped, rather like those of the primrose. The flower stalks grow out in pairs, where leaf and stem join. The flowers have four dark blue petals and grow in spikes.

Marsh Forget-me-not. Water side and damp places. Height nine to eighteen inches. Stems weak and slender, with narrow pointed leaves of delicate green, covered with minute hairs. The pale blue flowers, with a yellow centre, have five petals spread starwise. The small buds bear a pink colour, making the plant a most pleasing sight.

Lesser Periwinkle. April to September. In sheltered woods it sometimes flowers as early as February. Grows in woods and on shaded banks. Plant is a trailer. Stems round and long, from which the flower stalks stand six to ten inches high. The leaves are evergreen, oval in shape, and grow in pairs. The flowers are purple blue stars with white centres.

Germander Speedwell. June to August. Hedgerows. Height five to six inches. Stem is hairy and more or less prostrate. Hairy, rough, rounded leaves grow in pairs. The flowers form at the end of branches, and have four petals of clear blue, which encircle a white centre.

Chicory. July to September. Dry fields and hedgerows. Height two feet. Has erect, grooved, hairy stems,

8

and deeply serrated leaves. The flower head resembles a dandelion in shape, but is of a pale blue colour, and attached to the stem without a stalk.

MAUVE AND PURPLE FLOWERS

Heath. July to September. Moorlands. Height eight to twelve inches. Stems erect with small narrow leaves. Flowers are purple rosy bells, hanging mouth downwards. The blooms are much larger than the common heather or ling.

Heather, or Ling. July to September. Moor and heathlands. Height one to three feet. Stems are tough and woody, with numbers of small branches to which the small spiny leaves are attached. The flowers are reddish-purple, lilac and white. Individually they are tiny, but grow in numbers up the spikes and lie horizontally or even point upwards.

Black Knapweed. June to October. Meadow land and hedgerow banks. Height one to two feet. Stems stout and tough. Leaves are long, narrow and slightly indented. The flower heads are dark purple and somewhat resemble a thistle.

Scabious. June to August. Cornfields and meadows. Height two to three feet. Stems are strong, erect and covered with hairs. Delicate lilac flower heads about the size of half a crown are carried singly on the flower stalks

Wild Thyme. June to August. Dry banks. Height four to six inches. Has a woody stem, much branched, with small lance-shaped leaves growing in pairs. The small purple flowers appear at the tips of the short erect branches.

Wild Mint. July to August. Cornfields and hedgerow banks. Height eight to twelve inches. The stems are square with hairy serrated leaves growing in pairs, each pair being at right angles to those immediately below. The lilac flowers grow round the stems above the leaves. The plant has a strong scent.

Purple Loosestrife. July to September. Marsh ground and by the side of running water. Height two to five feet. Stems are tall, rigid and erect, with triangular, stalkless leaves. The flowers have reddish-purple petals and grow in rings round the stem, each ring forming above a pair of leaves. Perhaps a dozen of these flower groups will grow up the stem, decreasing in size as they approach the top.

Deadly Nightshade, or Belladonna. June to September. Chalky soil and stony ground. Height two to three feet. The stems are downy and branching. The leaves are oval in shape and grow in pairs; one leaf of each pair is small and one large. The bell-shaped flowers are a dull purple, sometimes streaked with yellow. Very poisonous. See p. 95.)

Woody Nightshade, or Bittersweet. June to September. Climbing on hedgerows. The woody stems are sometimes six feet in length, and carry pointed heart-shaped leaves. The flowers are purple with a yellow centre, and grow in drooping groups.

Wild Pansy. June to September. Cultivated fields. Height two to three inches. The stem is weak, and the leaves much divided. The flower, which is like a very small garden pansy, is a deep purple with the lower petals sometimes yellow, and occasionally the whole flower can be found of the same colour.

Sweet Violet. April to July. Woods and hedgerow banks. Height two inches. Stems are slender but strong, with flower stalks longer than the leaf stalks. The leaf is heart-shaped. The deep purple flowers are composed of two small petals above three larger ones, and have a delightful smell. The dog violets are of a paler purple colour, somewhat larger and without scent.

Common Bugle. June to August. Meadows and pasture lands. Has smooth creeping stems, but the hairy flower stalks rise six to twelve inches above them. The oval leaves grow in pairs, each pair at right angles to the pair below. The flowers vary in colour from blue, mauve to purple, and encircle the stem above each pair of leaves.

Common Mallow, or Rags and Tatters. June to September. Roadside and ditch. Height three to four feet. Hairy erect stem, with large, indented, kidney-shaped leaves. The lilac flowers have five petals, bearing distinct lines converging on the centre. These flowers grow on short stalks coming from the joints of leaves and main stem.

RED AND PINK FLOWERS

Poppy. July to September. Cornfields. Height one to two feet. Rough hairy stems with leaves deeply notched into segments. The flowers are large, with four soft scarlet petals, the bases of which are black.

Corncockle. June to September. Cornfields. Height two to four feet. Has an erect stem clothed with white hairs. The narrow leaves, sometimes four inches long, are rather like those of the surrounding corn. The flowers which appear singly on stalks coming from the joints of the upper leaves, are sometimes two inches across, and of a bright crimson-purple colour.

Red Valerian. May to August. On top of walls, railway embankments, and on cliffs. Height one to two feet. Stout green stems. The leaf has a broad base and tapers to a sharp point. The deep red flowers are very small, but are crowded together in rounded masses at the end of the stem.

Ragged Robin. May to August. Boggy ground and damp situations. Height two feet. Has erect, reddish, hairy stems, the upper part of which is rough and sticky. The narrow leaves are pale green and few in number. The bright rose flowers, with a darker centre, form loose clusters at the top of each stem, and have a ragged and untidy appearance.

Red Campion. April to August. Woodland clearings and sometimes on hedgerow banks. Height two feet. Hairy stout stems, with broad, oval, stalkless leaves also coated with hair. Flowers are usually dark pink. The five petals of the bloom are much divided, and give the appearance of ten petals. The white campion is a closely allied species.

Herb Robert. May to September. Wayside and edge of woods. Height twelve to fourteen inches. The stems, which are erect, slender, hairy, rather brittle and much branched, turn a rosy colour as they mature. The leaves are fernlike and graceful; bright green at first, changing to a deep red later. They possess an unpleasant smell. The flowers are small pink stars, in pairs on slender stalks.

Fumitory. April to June. Dry meadows and cornfields. Height one to two feet. Weak stems trail or climb. Leaves are greyish green, and resemble those of the fern. The tube-like flowers are rose-coloured tipped with crimson, and hang in numbers from the main flower stalk, which in turn springs from the side of the stem.

Red Deadnettle. All the year round. Cultivated land. Stem branched with spreading heart-shaped leaves, which are serrated. Pale reddish-purple flowers occur in clusters from the points of junction of leaves and stem.

Willow Herb, Rosebay, or Fireweed. July to August. On the verge of woods and copses. Height two to six feet. Leaves are narrow and long. Rose-pink flowers, about an inch in diameter, grow in numbers from the stems, and form a long loose head. The lower blooms open first; those at the top being last to appear. Very often you will find the feathered seed below with the newly opened flowers at the top. This plant has a number of close relations, of which the hairy willow herb is common in damp situations.

Dog Rose. June to August. Hedges. Climber. Leaves are broken up into five leaflets, and the flowers are composed of five sepals, pink and scented. The field rose is almost always white and scented.

Rest Harrow. June to September. Pasture lands. Generally creeps near the ground. The stem is hairy, and the leaves are composed of three leaflets. The flowers are pink in colour, and similar in appearance to the broom.

Scarlet Pimpernel. April to August. Cornfields and dry situations. Plant is a crawler, and the stems travel close to the ground. They are eight to twelve inches long, and are weak and much branched. The stalkless, oval leaves taper towards their points. The flowers are a coppery scarlet, have five petals and grow in pairs.

Section 19

GRASSES

It is a commonplace that the more we see of a thing, the less interest we take in it. This probably applies in a large measure to grass. We see it on all sides, we tread it underfoot in our walks, we remove it from our flower beds, and yet it is indispensable to our existence. The main source of our food is derived from grasses; in the Western Hemisphere wheat, and in the Eastern rice.

Without grass our supplies of meat, milk and butter would fail, as we should not be able to feed cattle or sheep.

In spring all grass looks the same, although we have over a hundred different kinds in the British Isles. With the summer the long narrow leaves appear, from which grow tubular stems supporting the flower clusters. These stems are divided into hollow, tough sections, the joints of which are solid and swollen.

Try and make a collection of the different grasses about July, press your specimens between blotting paper for a few days, and mount them on plain paper with fine strips of adhesive paper.

Grasses are most difficult to describe satisfactorily in the brief space at our disposal. Illustrations of the more common varieties are therefore given as the easiest way to identify them.

(1) *Yellow Oat Grass* is so named from the golden appearance of its crest, which stands up boldly in the meadow. June and July.

(2) *The Tall Oat Grass* is a much larger variety of the above. It is similar in appearance to oats, but the seeds are very much smaller. June and July.

(3) *Wild Oat*. As its name implies, this is the wild variety of our cultivated oats, and is of course smaller.

YELLOW OAT GRASS   TALL OAT GRASS   WILD OAT

(4) *Quaking Grass*. Found on chalky soils. It is of a distinctive appearance, as its little spikelets are continually on the move with the slightest breeze. June and July.

(5) *Meadow Foxtail* is easy to recognise from its close resemblance to a fox's brush. Can be seen in meadows from May onwards.

(6) *Crested Dog's Tail*. A feature of the downs and heavy soils. The serrated appearance of its flower head makes it quite distinctive. June onwards.

(7) *Wall Barley*. Has a bristly head resembling barley. Common by waysides from July onwards. Another allied kind with more slender heads is common in damp meadows.

(8) *Couch Grass* grows on arable and not as a rule on meadow land. The spikelets grow from all sides of the stem, which is round. July.

(9) *Perennial Rye*. The head is similar to couch grass in appearance, but the spikelets grow from two sides only of a flattened stem, which looks as if it had been crushed. June onwards.

(10) *Sweet Vernal*. It is to this grass that the smell of hay is chiefly due. May.

(11) *Cocksfoot* is a rough tall grass with a very conspicuous head. Grows well beneath trees. June onwards.

(12) *Barren Brome* has long stiff hairs to its spikelets. It is well named, because it flourishes on poor soils where little else will grow.

(13) *Annual Meadow Grass*. Does not grow to any great size, but is one of the first to flower. March.

(14) *Tall Fescue*. Frequently seen in meadows in July and August. Grows taller than most grasses, and should therefore be easy to identify.

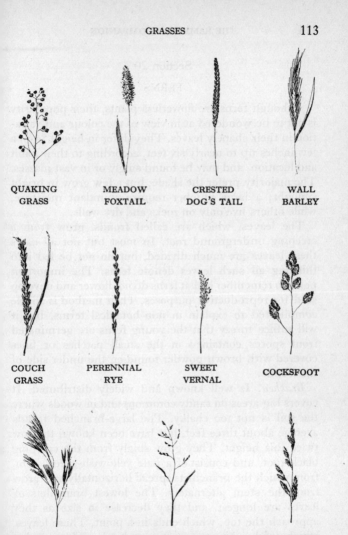

QUAKING
GRASS

MEADOW
FOXTAIL

CRESTED
DOG'S TAIL

WALL
BARLEY

COUCH
GRASS

PERENNIAL
RYE

SWEET
VERNAL

COCKSFOOT

BARREN BROME   ANNUAL MEADOW GRASS   TALL FESCUE

Section 20

FERNS

Although ferns are flowerless plants, their popularity is not to be wondered at in view of the colour and variation in their shapely leaves. They differ in height from a few inches up to nearly six feet, according to their habit and location, and may be found singly or in vast masses. The majority prefer the shade, but a few grow in bright sunlight; a large number require abundant moisture, while others live only on rocks and dry walls.

The leaves, which are called fronds, grow from a creeping underground root. In most but not all cases these leaves are much divided, but do not be led into thinking all such leaves denote ferns. The important point to remember is that ferns do not flower and develop seed for reproductive purposes. Their method is a little complicated to explain in non-botanical terms, but it will suffice to say that the young ferns are germinated from spores contained in the small patches or lines covered with brown powder found on the under side of the fronds.

Bracken. Is well known and widely distributed. It covers big areas on sandy commons and in woods where the soil is not too chalky. The large-branched fronds average about three feet, but have been known to grow twice this height. They grow singly from the creeping black root, and consist of a pale yellowish-green stem, from which the branchlets spread horizontally and grow from the stem alternately. The lowest branchlets or leaves are longest, and they decrease in size as they approach the top, which ends in a point. These leaves, which are bright green on top and pale and somewhat hairy underneath, are cut deeply into narrow segments. Bracken changes colour in the autumn, and where it exists in large tracts the sea of golden brown is very beautiful indeed. When dead and dry, the fronds make excellent bedding for animals. It is very difficult to eradicate once it has taken a hold on land, and frequent cutting seems to be the only hope. There are records of this fern in Elizabethan days.

The Male Fern. Has several fronds of two to four feet high, which rise more or less erect and in a circular group. They may be seen unrolling in early June. The general outline of the frond is not quite spear-shaped like bracken, as the two lowest leaflets are shorter than those above; it does, however, end in a point. The stalk is covered with a number of rough scales, but four-fifths of it bears branchlets. These are alternate, and are much the same width until they reach the top; they are divided into a large number of roundish blunt-toothed sections. The fern is plentiful in shady situations, and is one of the finest growing British varieties.

The Royal Fern. This is the most noble of all British ferns, and although not common, cannot be left out of any list. It is distinct from all others, and has a tuberous root which rises above the ground. The fronds rise from the crown of the root and are of two kinds, fertile fronds and barren fronds. The former are two to three feet high and few in number, but the latter are more numerous and rise to double the height of the fertile fronds. The stems are smooth and brown in colour, and have leaflets which are smooth and green in colour, and oblong and blunt in shape without toothed edges. The fertile fronds have, instead of the upper leaflets, a dense cluster of spore capsules, which are at first green, but ripen to reddish-brown. Prefers damp situations.

The Lady Fern. One of the most graceful of our ferns. The large brown root shows above ground, and the graceful fronds rise in a beautiful plume-like group from it. They are short and do not exceed eighteen inches in height; two-thirds of the stem bears leaflets and the remaining portion is covered with long scales. These leaflets are usually arranged alternately on the stem, are narrow and pointed and divided into a number of smaller much-toothed sections arranged opposite each other along the leaflet. This is the appearance of an average lady fern, but as it is of a very variable nature many different forms will be found.

Common Polypody Fern. Remains green in spite of frost and snow. Height from six to eighteen inches. One-third of the stalk is bare. The fronds are narrow and shaped like a spear head, and are divided into narrow strips on either side, the dividing space being deeply cut and extending nearly to the stalk.

The Common Maidenhair Spleenwort, or *English Maidenhair*. The fronds grow up to twelve inches in length, and consist of a smooth brown stalk on which are numerous dark-green leaflets of a blunt oblong shape, arranged opposite each other but decreasing in size as they approach the top of the stem. The leaflets run nearly to the bottom of the stem. Usually found in the hedge or on old walls.

Prickly Shield Fern. The numerous fronds are two to three feet high, and grow from the root in a circle. They are a dark bluish green, and somewhat paler underneath, in shape like a long narrow spear head. The leaflets grow to within a few inches of the base of the stem, which is covered with brown scales. They are rather close together, and unfold on the stem alternately and not opposite each other. The little leaves on the leaflets have irregular toothed edges, which are sharp and prickly. The fern is common in woods and on shady banks.

Hart's Tongue Fern. One of the commonest of our ferns, and distinct from all others. The fronds are smooth, bright green, long, narrow and pointed with an unbroken edge. The stem is covered with scales and has about one-third free from leaf. The fern grows from six to eighteen inches high.

Section 21

FUNGI

A fair amount of atmospheric heat and much moisture are the ideal conditions for fungi, and these requirements are usually met with in October and November, which are the best months to search for them.

It may be you are in the habit of making these little growths a target for your walking stick, but refrain for a moment, examine them, observe their curious shapes and beautiful colours, and perhaps you will find your interest sufficiently aroused to search for more. You will not find it a dry job, as many of the best specimens are to be found in damp woods, or in dripping under-growth.

It is not a collector's hobby, because few can be preserved, and even in our museums the best efforts of our experts can only run to thin sections or wax models. If, however, you can use a pencil, then you can sketch a collection indeed, or better still, the camera will provide you with even more accurate records.

Perhaps you are only vaguely interested however; then try and discover those varieties named in the following notes.

Sulphur Tuft Fungus. The name is descriptive, as it

has a round bright yellow cap with greenish gills surmounting a long thin stalk. As it grows old the centre of
the cap becomes brown and the gills tinged with purple.
This fungus grows in big clusters all the year round on
stumps and fallen trees. Very poisonous, and has an
unpleasant smell.

Striped Stump Flap Fungus. Varies from two inches to
twelve inches across. Grows on tree stumps. Variable in
colour, and upper side may be brown, grey or yellow,
striped with parallel lines; the under side of a white
or pale yellow. Woody in texture, with an unpleasant
smell.

Dryads Saddle Fungus. This has a pale buff upper
surface sprinkled with darker scales, and is white or grey
underneath. It grows sideways from the tree trunks, is
woody and often very large.

Common Elfcup. Small, rather like an irregular bird's
egg with a hole in it; greyish white outside and brown
inside.

Earth Star. Interesting and uncommon. Looks like a
dried-up starfish surmounted by a brown ball. Found in
damp woodlands.

Giant Puff Balls. Large white balls which need no
description.

Rough-Coated Puff Balls. Very much smaller than the
white puff ball, and has a rough darker exterior. The
white inside becomes gradually brown, and spores are
scattered through the open top when it bursts.

White Coral Tuft Fungus. Found in damp woods,
usually under hollies or firs. It has a pleasant smell, is
small, and resembles a piece of white coral.

Wrinkle Twig Fungus. About two to three inches high,
and has a dull fleshy twig-like growth.

Vegetable Tripe Fungus, or *Common Earthball*. When

young is a white or pale yellow, but it becomes darker and has a strong, rank smell as it grows older. The interior of the ball is blue-black at first, but gradually turns to a brown powder, and the ball splits irregularly at the top. At this stage they are known as snuffboxes, as when squeezed they emit a cloud of powdery spores, like snuff. Found in the woods, half buried in the ground. Distinguished from puffballs, which have a rounded hole in the top, through which the spores can be puffed by squeezing.

Giant Tuft Fungus. Uncommon but interesting. Grows at the foot of old tree stumps in a single clump of many branches, often measuring two to three feet across. The upper side varies in colour according to age, from bright brown to black; the under side is pale.

Jew's Ear Fungus. Occurs on fallen timber which lies among the damp herbage in the woods. In its early stages this fungus bears a remarkable resemblance to the human ear, but as it spreads with age, the likeness disappears. Soft and velvety to the touch, and flesh-coloured when young, this variety hardens and turns purple-black when dry. The purple colour is due to the spores scattered over the surface.

Pinky-cap Fungus. Grows singly in woods. It has a pale pinky-buff cap, and the gills have a rosy tinge and are broad and blunt.

Blenny Milk Mushroom. The cap is greyish and sometimes spotted; the flesh is hard and white. If the gills are bruised they become ashy grey, but if the fungus is broken, it exudes a white milky substance.

Blue-cap Fungus. Both cap and short stem are lilac blue. To be found in pastures in July to September, where it sometimes grows in rings.

Yellow Crack Boletus. Small olive-brown cap with

yellow cracks. The underside is a coarse yellowish fibre which changes to green, and the stem is yellow.

Edible Boletus. Common in woods and shady places from July to September. In appearance this fungus is fat and solid looking. The cap, which varies from buff to brown in colour, measures seven to eight inches across, and is white to yellow underneath.

The Parasol Mushroom. Bears its name because the ring round the stem can be moved up and down as on a parasol. It grows by the wayside and in woods.

Sickener Fungus. Rosy red cap sometimes fading to yellow, measures two inches across; gills white. The skin can be removed easily from the cap. A similar fungus, called the Sickener's Sister, measures less than two inches across, but has a tough adhesive skin. Both are poisonous.

Fly Agaric. Bright vermillion cap dotted with rough specks of white.

Common Inkcap Fungus. Has a smoky brown cap, which spreads out and melts into a black fluid when ripe.

Maned Inkcap. Has shaggy scales hanging down from its cap. It generally grows in groups, and like the common inkcap melts into an inky fluid when ripe.

The Oread are very small pale-coloured fungi, which spread themselves in fairy rings.

The Hairy Foot Fungus is pale coloured and rather like the oread in appearance. Grows in clumps on dead leaves. If the stem is pulled up, the bottom will be found to be covered in short hairs or bristles.

Common Cluster Fungus. Abundant on tree stumps and fallen trees. Has a small brownish cap on a long stalk, and grows in clusters. Appears as early as August.

Chameleon Fungus. Appropriately named, as it shows

great variation in colour, but is usually lilac or blue spotted with yellow.

Common Helvel. Frequent in woods and damp hedgerows. Although it has a cap, it has neither gills nor tubes; the spores are microscopic. The cap is pale brown but twisted and deformed-looking on a white irregular stem.

Sham Mushroom. The cap has a wavy outline and is clammy to the touch. The gills vary from white to dull grey, but are never pink, brown or purple like the edible mushroom. It has a rank smell.

Morel. Resembles a soiled piece of sponge on a short stem.

Small Stink Fungus. Small white stalk with a red point which grows from a white bulb-shaped base half buried in the ground. It may be handled while it remains white, but as it ripens and decays its smell becomes disgusting.

Stinkhorn Fungus. White stem about six inches long is surmounted by a wrinkled cap. Harmless when fresh, but smells offensively as it ripens.

Birds' Nest Fungus. Curious shape and extremely small. Commences as a short club-shaped growth which develops into a cone with a covered top. This subsequently breaks, and exposes a nest of button-like discs which contain the spores.

Chapter IV

NATURAL HISTORY

Section 22

ANIMALS

Deer. Although deer are the largest of our wild folk, they are some of the most inoffensive, as they are timid and rely for safety on their agility, speed, and a perfect sense of smell. The males carry antlers, which increase in size each year up to twelve. These antlers do not grow indefinitely, however, but drop off each winter and are succeeded in the spring by a larger set. The process is interesting, because as the antlers grow afresh from the skull they are covered with a fleshy layer of skin in which the blood circulates. When the growth is complete the blood ceases to circulate, and the skin or velvet, as it is called, dies and is rubbed off. When the antlers are clean, they are firmly fixed in the skull ready for fighting, and can only be separated by pulling off part of the skull. In the winter, however, a line of separation forms and they are knocked or rubbed off. There are three kinds of deer in Great Britain:

(1) Red Deer.
(2) Fallow Deer.
(3) Roe Deer.

Red Deer. Reddish brown in summer, greyish brown in winter, with a large white patch on the rump including the tail. The male is about forty-eight inches in height to the shoulder. The young are spotted with white. Deer have a solitary young one only, as a rule, and it is born in the spring. The antlers of the male make their appearance after seven months, but for the first two years are short and straight. The full-grown male, or stag, as he is called, at five years of age is the magnificent specimen so often portrayed in pictures of the Highlands.

The Fallow Deer. General colour yellowish brown with rows of white spots on the body, but sometimes uniform dark brown. The height of the male may be taken as roughly thirty-six inches. The antlers of the fallow deer are flattened and broad at the top, while those of the red deer are simply branch like.

The Roe Deer. Reddish brown in summer, greyish brown in winter, with a large white disc on the rump. Height of male, about twenty-four inches to the shoulder.

The Badger. Known by his friends as brock, the badger is the biggest and strongest of our wild animals with the exception of the deer. It is compact in build, short on the leg, with a fairly long snout, and in general outline not unlike a small bear. The head has long, conspicuous black and white stripes, which show up clearly against the grey-tipped brown of the body. The animal is a slow mover, but the short legs are extremely strong, and the feet have sharp claws specially adapted for digging. Its skin is very tough and loose, which enables it to turn round most unexpectedly if held—in fact, the only safe way to hold a badger is aloft by his tail, and you are not advised to try this unless you are very experienced, because the teeth are sharp and workmanlike. The badger feeds mainly on roots, berries and insects, and does not do as much damage as is attributed to him. It becomes very fat in autumn before retiring to the snug recesses of its home or "earth," which consists of a central, living chamber situated out of all draughts and adjoining a storage compartment in which grass and herbage are kept. These quarters are situated at the end of a long tunnel with various galleries leading in all directions, and an old earth may extend as much as a hundred yards. Badgers move by night, and are therefore little known. They mate for life, and have two or three cubs in the spring.

The Otter. Not by any means rare, but is shy, and its nocturnal habits keep it from observation. It is a little over two feet in length, and weighs on average about twenty pounds. The fur is blackish and soft, and is not only almost waterproof, but does not offer any resistance when swimming. The tail is long and flattened, and the legs short with webbed feet armed with sharp claws. The teeth are sharp and particularly well adapted to hold a slippery fish. The otter is fierce and strong for its size, and a perfect, soundless swimmer, both on the surface and below; resembling a great eel when under water. The animal is a great traveller, sometimes proceeding to the sea down the tideway in search of food, or going overland to some new stream or river. Two or three young are born in the spring in some hole in the bank. They are quite blind, and remain so for nearly three months. After this period they are taken to the water and taught to swim by their parents, as, curiously enough, they are not natural swimmers. However, they soon take to the water and learn to forage for themselves.

The Fox. A well-formed animal, with reddish fur, broad head, sharp nose and bushy tail. It has keen sight and highly developed senses of smell and hearing. Extremely cunning, and possessing a great power of endurance, the fox exists in far larger numbers than is generally imagined. It is, however, nocturnal in habit, and passes unnoticed in the darkness. Not infrequently foxes are surprised on country roads by the sudden appearance of the headlights of a car, and can be seen for a few seconds before springing into the hedge for cover. The animal possesses a most unsavoury smell, by which it can be traced, or at any rate some of its haunts discovered. The fox is very regular in habit and returns to the same hunting-ground again and again, observing a fairly accurate time-table. Although not despising an occasional rat, the favourite food consists of poultry, game and similar delicacies, and a great deal of damage is done by the animal, as it unfortunately kills wholesale if among poultry, and without regard to its possible consumption. The fox hides by day in a hole, called its earth, and for this purpose he may enlarge the dwelling of a rabbit, or thrust himself upon the badger. The cubs are born underground about April. They are usually black at birth, and open their eyes after fourteen days. Probably you will have a better opportunity of seeing the cubs than the parents, because the vixen usually takes them to a little open-air playground, where they play like kittens, oblivious for the moment of the hard struggle for existence to come.

The Rabbit. Is familiar to all. The ears have no black tips, and are shorter than those of the hare. The hare also possesses longer hind legs, and the movement of the rabbit is therefore more even. Its erect white tail is a noteworthy feature when seeing the animal on the run to its burrow, where it retreats on alarm. It breeds frequently during the year, increases with astounding rapidity, and would undoubtedly become a plague but for its many enemies, chief of which is man. The young are born blind, and without fur.

The Hare. Does not go to ground like the rabbit, but lives in the open. It relies entirely on its speed for safety, but unless wounded or hurt, with the aid of its long hind legs it can usually outdistance its pursuers and reach safety. They run much more rapidly uphill than down. Rabbits live in colonies, but the hare is solitary. Hares have three or four litters in a year, and the young are born with their eyes open. "As mad as a March hare" is a proverbial saying, but the madness is merely the grotesque antics of courtship.

The Hedgehog. At twilight on a summer evening the hedgehog may be seen padding his way along the country lane or the wood clearing. It will be seeking snails, frogs, mice, beetles or worms, and be away before dawn, because it is nocturnal in its habits. Occasionally eggs will be taken, but generally speaking the hedgehog is beneficial to mankind, as it eats an enormous number of troublesome insects. It has an armour of spines, which afford a certain amount of protection, because on the approach of danger it can roll itself into a ball, the head, legs and tail being completely hidden.

The Stoat. About twelve inches long and of a reddish-brown colour, with a clear black tip to the tail and white under the body. If you feel a difficulty in deciding whether an animal is a stoat or a weasel, remember that the latter is much smaller and the black tip to the stoat's tail is conclusive. In the north the stoat changes his coat in the winter to white, and becomes an ermine, but this change is not so usual in the warmer south. The life of the animal is one of unending murder by killing hares, rabbits and similar quarry. If you find a dead rabbit with tooth-marks in the neck, you may be sure you have a stoat's kill, and that the unfortunate bunny has been sucked dry of its blood before being left. Possessing a marvellous faculty of scenting its prey and tremendous patience, coupled with swiftness and the ability to climb, the stoat is an unequalled huntsman. Although ferocious, they have the one redeeming feature of playfulness, and their antics in their few times of leisure are a joy to see. They rear one family every year, usually in April.

The Weasel. The habits of the weasel are similar in every way to its big cousin, the stoat. In size it may be some eight inches long, and similar in colour, but the black tail tip is absent. In addition, weasels do not change to white in winter. Being small, the animal can use the underground burrows of mice, and they form his staple diet. Thus he is rather a friend of man than an enemy, but he suffers for the misdemeanours of the stoat and is killed ruthlessly. Several families are born during the year.

The Red Squirrel. The most graceful and agile of our wild animals. It is a fine red chestnut colour, with a white chest and a huge feathery tail carried along the back. The head and body are about eight inches long, and the tail is the same length. The squirrel is a charming sight scampering from branch to branch, but it is nervous when on the ground, and rarely makes a journey any distance overland. The nest, or dray, as it is called, is domed and has a small hole for entrance. In such a nest, or in a hole in the tree, a family numbering four will be born in July. The animal feeds on nuts, beech mast, fir cones and berries. It usually buries a certain amount of food for winter use. The red squirrel is disappearing before the gradual advance of his cousin the grey squirrel, which was first imported into the London parks.

The Grey Squirrel. Is bigger and stronger than the red. It is hardier and better able to survive long-continued bad weather. A fierce fighter, it is called by some "the tree rat," and does an enormous amount of damage to crops and bird life. The small red squirrel is quite unable to resist it, and disappears as the grey advances.

The Mole. Larger than a mouse, but smaller than a rat. It has a soft sleek coat of dull leaden black, which is not soiled by earth, and will set either way to facilitate slipping backwards and forwards. The head is narrow and small, with scarcely discernible eyes and a long snout for pushing through loose earth. The mole has short legs and paws specially strengthened for digging. A feeble tail and dwindling sight represent the dis-appearance of organs not required; the sense of smell and hearing are, however, very acute. In March and April their presence can be ascertained by many little mounds dotted about the grass. If one of the larger mounds is opened it will be found to contain a central chamber, with a nest of coarse grass lined with finer grass; from this central room many side passages lead off to feeding grounds. The mole comes to the surface a good deal at two seasons of the year; in the early part because his burrows are waterlogged, and in the summer because the drought hardens the ground and makes digging difficult. Caterpillars provide a useful addition to his diet at this time.

The Water Vole. Commonly called the water rat. The fur is a dark, rich brown. About eight inches long, of stout build, but with short ears and tail. Lives by the water side, and is a good swimmer. In winter, the floods may drive the little creature on land. A vegetarian and harmless.

The Rat. Is well known, but it may be useful to dis-tinguish from his harmless relative the water vole, or water rat. The rat has big ears and long tail; the water vole has short ears and short tail. The rat is bigger and of a grey colour, while the vole is a dark, rich brown.

The Field Vole. Called also the short-tailed field mouse. About five inches in length, including a short hairy tail of about an inch; the ears are also short. In spite of the fact that field voles are kept down in numbers by owls and kestrels, they frequently become a plague.

The Mouse. Needs no description. Remember, however, that his long ears and long bare tail distinguish him from the vole.

Long-Tailed Field Mouse. Much smaller than an ordinary mouse. Reddish brown in colour and whitish underneath. Has a large lustrous black eye. Makes a nest on the corn stalks.

The Common Shrew. Blackish grey, tinged with brown on the back, and paler underneath. The fur is soft, short and silky, the ears small and the snout long and tapering. The animal measures about four inches from the tip of its snout to the end of its tail, the pigmy shrew, which is the smallest of our mammals, being an inch shorter. It is braver than its size warrants, because of a peculiar smell which renders it immune from attack by other wild folk in search of food. However, cats are known to kill shrews in large numbers, but never to eat them. Worms and caterpillars are the usual diet, and the little creatures do not burrow, but live in dense herbage. They are of ancient origin, and their teeth are tipped with red.

Section 23

BIRDS AND THEIR NESTS

Ramblers' interests will vary, and to many flowers and trees will appeal because they abound and can be examined at leisure. If, however, you are quick of eye and observant, you will find the study of birds absorbing.

The following notes do not pretend to deal comprehensively or scientifically with the subject, but are given to enable you to identify a few common species and their nests. Many varieties of colour occur, due to age, sex and various natural causes. Space will not permit details of these to be given, but you may take the description to cover the general appearance, and to enable an average person to identify an average bird.

No scientific terms have been used, or scientific classification attempted, but the colour method adopted seems the most convenient for the uninitiated reader. If you see a black-coloured bird, obviously the quickest way to find something about it is to turn to the section dealing with birds of dark plumage.

If you pursue the study patiently, you will obtain a good deal of information from watching birds with the aid of field-glasses, and no doubt will turn to a well-illustrated text-book. There are many sides to examine, and if you are in earnest, each will be found complete in itself and provide opportunities for research. The problems of plumage and its variation, nesting habits, food, flight and migration are legion, and will furnish you with a hobby of countless possibilities if approached with patience, sympathy and an insatiable curiosity.

Dark or Black Plumage, Black and White or Blue and White Birds

The Rook. Nesting operations commence at the end of February, and the nests, usually in colonies, are placed at the top of elms and other high trees. The birds generally return to the same rookery year after year and repair their old nest. These nests are large, open-shaped structures, composed of a great number of sticks and twigs, carefully built, plastered with mud and lined with straw and hay. Four to five eggs are laid, and are of a bluish-green colour spotted with dull brown. The birds have a glossy black ill-fitting plumage, and the old ones have a grey featherless patch round the beak. Rooks usually walk with a solemn preoccupied air.

The Crow. Is often confused with the rook, but is not difficult to distinguish. They are about the same size as rooks, but go about in pairs, whereas the rooks rove in numbers. The crow is entirely black, hops more than walks, and has an alert attitude. It builds a solitary nest on a fork or branch high in a tree. This large, cup-shaped nest, strengthened with mud, contains four to five eggs of a sea-green colour spotted with brown. Crows are extremely cunning and destructive, and do much harm to game and poultry.

The Jackdaw. Smaller than a crow and about the size of a pigeon. Plumage glossy black at the side of the head and back of the neck. In character alert and very mischievous. Builds in holes in cliffs, in ruins, under roofs and similar places. Makes a very untidy nest of miscellaneous material, but lines it with wool and feathers. Lays four to five eggs in May, of pale blue with deep brown and black spots.

The Raven. Uncommon. A large black bird with ample glossy plumage and powerful beak, and murderous in the extreme. They are early builders but very rarely use trees, preferring cliffs and similar inaccessible places. The nest is composed of a large quantity of twigs lined with moss. Four to six eggs are laid, of a bluish-green blotched with dark brown.

The Blackbird. Is glossy black with a yellow bill, and the female is deep brown. On the ground it hops and runs, but in the air it has a strong flight, and cocks its tail on alighting. Its nest, in hedges and bushes, usually about five feet from the ground, is easy to find, being cup-shaped, lined with mud, and finished inside with grass.

Two or three broods are brought up in a year, and the eggs, about five in number, are sea green, flecked with cinnamon.

The Starling. In full plumage the male is very handsome in his blackish feathers, with pale spangles glossed with purple and green. The birds have a somewhat brownish appearance in winter, which the female never loses. The nests, which are made in holes, in cliffs or houses, are sometimes composed of an enormous amount of material, and contain four to five pale blue, unmarked eggs. The first brood are chased from the nest unmercifully to make way for the second brood, and these homeless youngsters join the vast flocks to be seen in winter, while the old birds still remain in their nest-home.

The Swallow. Bright brown forehead and throat ; crown of the head, upper part, and a band on chest, of deep metallic blue; buff underneath. Has a swift skimming flight. The nest is of mud and straw, lined with feathers, and is constructed near the roof or on the eaves. Lays four to six eggs, which are white, speckled with grey and brown, and raises two broods annually.

The Martin. Upper part of head, back and tail glossy blue-black; wings black, and under part white with white feathers covering legs and toes. Similar to a swallow in flight. Makes a mud nest lined with feathers, but it can be distinguished from that of the swallow by the absence of straw. The nest is enclosed, and has a small entrance hole. Martins raise two broods in a year, and lay four to five pure white eggs. They often return to the same nest for many years.

The Swift. Blackish-brown with a bronze lustre and a small grey patch under the chin. It is fast in flight, and is nearly always on the wing, but when on the ground it has a crawling gait. It produces two white eggs in June, and the nest of hay and wool is matted together with a secretion from the birds.

The Magpie. Black with a white shoulder patch; the throat is black with a white front and underbody; tail and wings very dark purplish blue. The whole effect is a very handsome black and white appearance. Magpies are cunning, lively, chattering birds, not quite as big as a rook. The nest is large and domed, and is made of sticks cemented together by clay and mud, the whole being protected outside by thorn twigs. Six to seven eggs are produced about May, and are of a pale green speckled with grey and brown. The birds pair for life, and return to the same nest high up in a tree, adding more sticks each season.

Drab-coloured Birds

The Song Thrush. The upper parts are olive brown, and the throat and breast buff speckled with brown. A good songster, found in gardens, woods and hedges. Rears two broods annually, and makes first nest in March. The deep cup-shaped nest of twigs and grass, with its hard lining of mud, is usually placed in hedges, bushes and trees, about five feet from the ground. The eggs are bright blue marked with black spots, and number from four to six. The thrush is called the mavis in Scotland.

The Skylark. Somewhat larger than a sparrow. Brown, speckled on back of neck and breast. Lighter brown underneath, with white edges to tail. Rises somewhat slowly with a laboured flight, but may be easily recognised in the air on a summer day, hovering in the sky and giving out its peaceful song. The lark exhibits a slight crest when alarmed. The eggs are difficult to find, as the bird alights some distance from them, and runs along the ground unobserved. The nest, which is on the ground in high grass or corn, is loosely made of hay and grass, and contains four to five eggs of pale green thickly spotted with dark brown.

The House Sparrow. Rears several broods in a year. It is grey on top of the head and bottom of the back. The main part of the back is brown with one white stripe, and another small white stripe is to be seen over the eye. The cheek, side of neck and underneath are white, while the breast and throat are black. The nest, which is made of straw, grass or hay, thickly lined with feathers, may be found in a great variety of places—tree stumps, hedges, bushes, outhouses, and even gutterings. Lays five to six eggs, which vary greatly in colour, but are frequently pale bluish white, speckled with brown.

The Tree Creeper. Common at all seasons of the year, but is not very noticeable on account of its small size and colour, which is brown on the head and wings, and grey beneath. The bird is shy, and only takes short flights from tree to tree. The tree creeper is well named, because it does actually creep up tree trunks in search of insects in the bark, and in so doing might at first sight be almost mistaken for a mouse. Pursuing a peculiar spiral route, it holds by its claws, and is supported by its long tail, while the slender curved beak is well adapted to search crevices for insects, but is not strong enough to tear the bark. About April six to nine white eggs with red speckles are laid in a small cup-shaped nest of fine grass lined with wool and feathers, inside a crevice or hole.

The Linnet. Smaller than a hen sparrow. Usually brown, but colour varies; sometimes reddish brown in males and greyish brown in females. Can be distinguished from sparrows and similar birds by the pale grey colour on the tail, and the peculiar rising and falling flight. It has a hard conical bill, and always goes in flocks. Five to six eggs are laid of a bluish-white colour marked with deep brown spots and streaks. The nest is made of small twigs and dry grass lined with wool and hair, and is of the open cup-shaped type. Linnets will occasionally build in small groups, some of the nests being quite close to each other.

Brightly Coloured Birds

The Jay. Has a grey crest speckled with black. The back is brown with a white patch at the tail end; the wings are black and white with a distinctive barred band of bright blue feathers; the body is cinnamon and the tail black. Jays are to be seen in the woodlands, and are often discovered by their peculiar harsh cry, or, if on the wing, by an unusual bobbing flight, the bird rising and falling with each wing movement. The deep cup-shaped nest made of twigs, with a thick lining of grass and hair, is made in thick cover about five or six feet from the ground. Four to five greenish-grey eggs dotted with dull brown are laid in April or May.

The Green Woodpecker. The largest and most brightly coloured of our woodpeckers. The upper part is a deep olive green, and the underneath pale greyish green; the crown of the head and neck are red and the sides of the face black with a white mark. The woodpecker never perches, but runs up trees in a spiral direction, supported by its tail feathers. It never descends in this manner, but flies down. The birds peck a hole in the rotten part of a tree, and after going in a short distance construct a chamber about a foot deep. It is unlined, and contains five to eight pure white eggs, which are laid during April and May.

The Robin. Well known by all. The upper part and wings are brown, the breast red bordered with bluish grey, and the lower breast and under part white. It is to be seen a great deal on the ground, where it hops. The nest is composed of moss, grass and dead leaves, and lined with hair. The robin sometimes chooses some extra-ordinary places in which to build; an old tin can, flower-pot or some similar article may be selected quite near a house, in preference to a hole in the bank or the roots of a tree. Two or three broods are raised each year, and the eggs, about five in number, are creamy white streaked with reddish brown.

The Bullfinch. The cock is a familiar sight and easily recognised. He is solid looking and sturdy, with a rosy breast, black hood extending below the beak, black wings with a white bar, and a black tail. The back is grey with the exception of a white patch by the tail. The females are not quite so brightly coloured on the breast, and are brown on the back. The birds have a dipping flight, and bring up two broods in a year, the first in April or May. The nest is built in bushes and hedges, and is a neat cup-shaped structure, placed on a platform of twigs and roots. The eggs are greenish blue marked with spots of purple and lilac, and number five or six.

The Great Tit. About the size of a sparrow but slimmer in build. Has a black top to the head with white cheeks and a white smudge on the nape of the neck; the wings are black; the back is greenish blue, and the breast yellow with a distinct black strip down the middle. The eggs number about ten, and are white blotched with red. These birds build in holes, but insist in filling all the vacant space with moss, on top of which the neat round nest of grass, hair and feathers is placed. Great tits are very pugnacious and murderous. They kill other small birds for the pleasure of eating their brains, and leave the remainder of their victims untouched.

The Blue Tit. Similar in colour to the great tit, but much smaller. Full of fight, and not afraid of human beings. Nests in April in a hole in the wall, or some similar spot, and lays eight to ten speckled white eggs.

The Woodpigeon. Bluish-grey head with side and neck glossed with green and violet. Has a small patch of white each side of the neck. The back is brown and grey; the wings grey edged with white, and the breast rich lustrous purple. Pigeons are strong in flight and may be seen roosting in large numbers on trees. They usually build high in the branches, the nest being a mere platform of twigs loosely put together. Two white eggs are laid, and two or three broods are brought up in a year. The cock sits by day and the hen by night.

The Hawfinch. Twice the size of a sparrow, with a big beak and a white ring round the eyes. It has a brown cap and back, blue-grey marking in nape of neck, and black wings with large white patches. The cheeks and breast are reddish in colour, and the tail a mixture of white, black and brown. The females are not quite so highly coloured, but there is no mistaking them, as they are very conspicuous in flight, but do not go in flocks. The nest is cup-shaped, something like that of the bullfinch, and is lined with fine roots, grass and hair. The site, however, varies, and they may be found sometimes in the hedge, and sometimes quite high in a tree. Four to six eggs of pale grey with brown spots and blotches may be found from May onwards.

The Goldfinch. One of the most beautiful and smallest of our finches. Easily distinguished by its bright colours; the side of the head is red with a white margin, the wings are black and deep yellow, and the body is reddish fawn. There is very little difference in colouring between the cock and the hen. The goldfinch may be seen in fields

10

and waste land in autumn feeding on thistle heads, groundsel, and the seeds of other troublesome weeds. Its pointed beak is specially suitable for this work. The cup-shaped nest is made as early as May and sometimes as late as July, and is usually fairly high up in an apple or cherry tree, but it does not despise an oak or a beech. The eggs, which number from four to five, are bluish white, marked with reddish-brown spots and lines.

The Chaffinch. Is a little more slender than a sparrow, but has a well-defined white pattern on its black wings, and no other white on its body. The male has a black forehead, pink breast and a black tail. Chaffinches fly in flocks, and make very neat nests in shrubberies, hedges or in the fork of a fruit tree. In April or May four to five eggs of purplish grey with dark brown markings are laid in the smooth, open, cup-shaped nest, which is decorated on the outside with moss.

The Yellowhammer. The male has both head and throat bright yellow, chest and underneath paler yellow with brown streaks, wings and back brown with black markings, and a bright chestnut patch above the blackish tail. The female carries very little yellow, and the streaks on her face are blackish. Makes a neat nest in April, which consists of dry roots and moss, lined with fine grass and hair. The four to five eggs vary from white to pale mauve with brown shadings streaked with hair-like markings of deep purplish red, sometimes nearly black.

The Greenfinch. A little larger than a sparrow. The male can be distinguished by its greenish colour and yellow edge to the wing. The female is more brown and shows very little yellow. The greenfinch lives in flocks and nests in hedges or trees, two or more nests sometimes being together. The untidy nest of twigs, roots and moss is lined neatly and firmly. Four to five very pale blue eggs spotted with brown are laid.

The Nuthatch. Somewhat smaller than a sparrow, but with a larger head and long bill. Grey back, buff beneath, with chestnut flanks and a black eye stripe from beak to ear. It has a peculiar elongated powerful first toe, which enables it to run down tree trunks head first as easily as it climbs. Its tail is short, for the same reason. The nuthatch has a strong pointed beak, which it uses to split nuts. The eggs are white with reddish-brown spots, and number five to eight.

Water Birds

The Kingfisher. A shy but not uncommon water bird, which rarely leaves the water side. It is perhaps the most handsomely coloured of all British birds, although somewhat unshapely and ill-proportioned, with an exceedingly long beak. The top of the head, wings, tail and line from eyes to wings are all lustrous dark greenish blue, slightly mottled. The back is of a somewhat paler blue, the throat white, and the under part chestnut. It nests in a hole in the bank, sometimes two or three feet long, and the end is widened to form a chamber, which is without lining. The young, however, have a habit of ejecting pellets of undigested food, which is gradually trodden into a kind of mat. Six to nine almost round glossy white eggs are laid during May and June. The bird may sometimes be seen sitting motionless on a branch, from which it will dart suddenly forward to catch a fish, swallowing it head first. Usually it will be seen flying swiftly over the surface of the water.

The Heron. A large bird about three feet long. The crest is bluish black, and the upper part of the body slate grey. The forehead is white, and also the neck, which carries two long dark streaks ending in a plume of long white feathers hanging down in front. The under part and long legs are both grey, and the bill yellow. The bird has a slow stately walk, something like a stork, and wades in search of fish, spears them with its long bill, and carries them ashore to eat. It builds in colonies at the top of high trees. The large rough nest of sticks, lined with grass, rests on a kind of platform, and contains three to five pale greenish-blue eggs. Herons usually return to the same nest every year and rear two broods, the first in February or March.

The Moorhen. Has a red bill with a yellow tip; the head, neck and under part being dull grey with some white streaks on the sides; the back and upper parts are dark brown. The bird runs and swims with a bobbing motion of the head, and frequently dives under the water. The large open nest of reeds and grass is usually placed among the reeds and rushes. Moorhens lay seven to ten buff eggs speckled with deep brown. Two broods are raised annually, and the young of the first brood have the singular habit of feeding and helping to rear the second brood.

The Wild Duck. There are many kinds of wild duck, the best known of which is the mallard. Its head and neck are glossy green, with a narrow white ring at the bottom of the neck. The back and breast are chestnut, the under part pale grey, with greenish-black wings carrying two white stripes. The female is not so handsomely coloured as her mate, and is of a mottled brown colour. Mallards are powerful and rapid in flight; they spend the day on the water, and usually fly by night. The nest is made on the ground near water, and is composed of rushes, leaves and dry grass, lined with down plucked from the breast of the female. Eight to twelve pale green eggs are laid during March and April.

Game Birds

The Pheasant. About three feet in length, including the long tail, which is one of its most distinctive features. Red round the eyes; a metallic blue neck, at the bottom of which is a white ring. The male bird has brilliant spangled brown and copper plumage, often displaying a green lustre. The female is brown, barred with black. Easily recognised in flight, as it is very rapid, with tail straight out and producing a loud whirring sound. The nests, made in April, are of dried grass lined with leaves, and are to be found in a hollow in the ground. The eggs are olive brown, and number ten to fourteen. The pheasant runs swiftly along the ground, but roosts in trees.

The Partridge. Size about twelve inches. Has a bright chestnut head and a grey throat. The back and wings are brown, speckled with black, and if it is possible to make a fairly close examination, you distinguish the male by a brown horseshoe mark low down on the breast. The partridge is rapid in flight, but does not rise high, often just skimming the tops of the hedges. It sleeps on the ground, and lives in coveys, but pairs for breeding in February. The nests are made in the long grass or bottom of the hedge, and ten to twenty olive-brown eggs are produced.

The Woodcock. About the size of a pigeon, with a long beak. The upper plumage is reddish brown marked with black, and the breast and under parts are light brown marked with an even paler shade of the same colour. The nest is composed of dried leaves and grass placed in some hollow in the woods. Four to five eggs are laid, which are buff coloured, marked with light brown spots and grey patches. The bird rests during the day, but at dusk and early morning follows a well-defined path in the undergrowth to and from its feeding ground.

Section 24

BUTTERFLIES AND MOTHS

The life of a butterfly or moth consists of four stages:

(a) The egg.
(b) The caterpillar.
(c) The chrysalis.
(d) The perfect and completed insect.

(a) *The Egg*. The eggs are small, generally about the size of a pin's head, and an examination by means of a magnifying glass will reveal the fact that many different shapes and varieties exist. These eggs are usually deposited by the female on plants, shrubs and trees, which are to provide the future foodstuff of the caterpillar. They resemble little seeds adhering to the food plant, frequently under the leaf.

(b) *The Caterpillar*. The eggs hatch out in periods which vary from a few weeks to several months, and the young caterpillar, or larva as it is called, commences to feed at once, usually making a start on the eggshell. Growing rapidly, it changes its skin several times before becoming fully grown. Caterpillars vary greatly in size, colour, and appearance, some being hairy, some with a few hairs, and others entirely smooth.

(c) *The Chrysalis*. When fully grown, the caterpillars prepare for one of their most important changes into the chrysalis or pupa. The operation is sometimes complicated, and involves various methods of fixing themselves to the plant by hooks, belts or thread, or, alternatively, burying themselves in the ground. In all cases the caterpillar becomes more and more inactive, and gradually changes into an inert case, sometimes coloured and suspended from the plant, sometimes buried in the earth. They remain in this condition for varying periods, some varieties for a few weeks only, others over the whole winter.

(d) *The Perfect Insect*. When the change inside the chrysalis is complete and the time comes to emerge, the insect splits the chrysalis case, and shakes itself free from the shell. At this stage it appears damp with the wings dwarfed and deformed. It soon dries, however, and the wings assume their full size.

THE DIFFERENCE BETWEEN BUTTERFLIES AND MOTHS

There is no month in the year in which you will not discover some butterfly or moth on the wing. Naturally the majority are to be seen in the summer, which is Nature's most prolific period, but many remain well into the autumn, and a few even in December to cheer us at the dying of the year.

To many they are just butterflies or moths, and there seems to be great confusion of thought as to whether a particular specimen comes within one category or the other. This is excusable to some extent when it is considered that there are in Great Britain some sixty varieties of butterflies and over two thousand different moths.

Some of the butterflies are rare, or local, and many of the moths extremely small, but it is evident that any attempt at classification, with or without the use of scientific terms, would be a lengthy undertaking. Certain of the more common varieties have therefore been dealt with in the following notes, which it is hoped will encourage the reader to pursue his inquiries further, both in the field and in some well-illustrated and reliable text-book.

The most certain mark of distinction between British butterflies and moths is that the former have their thread-like antennæ, or horns, clubbed at the end, while the thicker feelers of moths vary from pointed horns to feathery appendages.

Broadly speaking, butterflies rest with their wings raised over their backs in a perpendicular position, the under side of the wings being of a neutral tint for protection against birds and other enemies.

In many cases both the front and rear wings of butter-flies are brightly coloured, while a large number of moths bear bright colours on one pair of wings only. This is again a measure of protection, as the majority of moths rest with their wings horizontal, the neutral-coloured forewings covering the brightly coloured back members. If the forewings bear the colour, it is probable that it will match in some inexplicable fashion the food plant on which the moth rests.

In general, it will be found that the bodies of butterflies are thinner and more shapely than those of moths.

Finally, more moths fly at dusk or in the evening than by day. You will find exceptions, but the foregoing remarks will give you a broad distinction which experience will develop.

Butterflies

The Large White. Well known in town or country. Both sexes are creamy white with black tips to the forewings, but the female can be distinguished from the male by two black spots on each front wing. Large numbers of eggs are laid, and this butterfly causes considerable damage to the market gardener. The eggs are laid in great numbers on the under-side leaves of the food plant. Found May to September, but rare during July.

The Small White. Even more numerous than its bigger relative. Cream or creamy yellow with faint black tips to the forewings. The male has one black spot on each of its forewings and one on each of its lower wings, but occasionally the former may be unmarked. The female, on the other hand, has two distinct black spots on her forewings, and one on each of the lower wings. It is interesting to note that these whites are a variation from the usual rule of the males bearing the more distinct marks and colouring. Can be found April to September. Rare in July.

The Brimstone. Hibernates and can be seen on the wing early in the year. The male is of a rich yellow, but the female is much paler with almost a green tinge. All four wings in both sexes bear a single deep orange spot.

The Comma. The wings are so irregular in outline that at first sight they give the impression of a very battered and torn insect. Closer examination will show that the scalloped edges of the wings are regular and rather beautiful. The basic colour is a golden orange with brown margins to the wings and a series of regular black spots. The reverse side of the wings is greeny brown, but on the under side the rear wing has a distinct white sign resembling a comma, which gives the insect its name.

The Small Tortoiseshell. One of the best known and best looking of our butterflies. An area of bright brown surrounds the body, followed on the forewings by a patch of deep orange, with alternate wide yellow and black stripes on the front of the wings. The hind wings have their area of brown with a wide orange stripe round the wing, followed by that most distinctive feature of all, a series of bright blue crescents. The small tortoisehell is amazingly brightly coloured. Seen on the wing it is somewhat smaller than other butterflies of this type, and may be easily recognised by the blue edging to its hind wings. When resting with the dull under sides only showing it is practically invisible. Found from July onwards; sometimes hibernates during the winter and appears again early in the year.

The Peacock. Another unmistakable and beautiful species. The basic colour of the wings is brownish red. On each hind wing it carries round blue circles resembling the marks on a peacock's tail. A yellowish-red circle framed in black can be seen on the front part of each forewing. Usually first seen in March.

The Red Admiral. Has the habit of sunning itself by gently flapping its wings backwards and forwards, and is a most impressive sight when doing this on the nettles. It is mainly a very deep brown, almost black, with vivid red straps crossing each forewing, and a few distinctive small white patches above. The hind wings have broad red borders, with a row of small black spots along each. May be seen from June, and often up to October.

The Meadow Brown. One of the most abundant of our butterflies, and may be seen in June, July and August. The male is dark brown with a white-centred black spot encircled with orange on each forewing. The female is more brightly coloured. It carries the same spot as the male, but the forewings carry a wide patch of orange. The hind wings sometimes carry a little shaded orange. The spots on the wings are equally distinct on the under sides.

The Common Blue. Plentiful from May to October. The male is blue or mauvy blue, with a narrow edge of black on the wings and narrow black veins. The female is brown with a border of orange spots on the forewings, and a border of black and orange spots on the hind wings. The under sides are very beautiful, the male being grey and the female pale brown spotted with white rings containing a black centre, and with a spotted orange border to each wing.

The Small Heath. Found almost everywhere from May to September. It is of a pale brown colour on all wings with a narrow greyish-brown border and a small single black spot towards the tip of each forewing.

The Small Copper. Can be seen from April to September. Forewings of a bright metallic orange with a broad brown border and a variable number of black spots. The hind wings are dull brown bordered by bright orange, the border containing a number of small black spots.

Moths

The Poplar Hawk. This is one of the hawk moth family, most of which are large with conspicuous caterpillars carrying a horn on their tails. The poplar hawk varies somewhat in its colourings, but is usually grey with a wide brown central band on its forewings, containing a single white spot. There is a well-defined red patch at the base of the hind wings. The body is large, and the wings when extended measure about three inches across. This moth appears in May or June.

The Puss Moth. This moth is fairly common, but its caterpillar is particularly interesting. The head and body of the insect are fluffy, and the latter is marked by clear black bands. The wings are whitish and crossed by many wavy black lines. It is about three inches from wing tip to wing tip. The caterpillar is green with a purple band or saddle down the back edged with yellow. The head is brown with an outside ring of black, and the section behind is green margined with yellow and having two black spots. When alarmed the caterpillar will withdraw its head into the section behind and the black spots assume the appearance of eyes, making it look most grotesque and to some terrifying, although it is of course quite harmless.

The Buff Tip. Front wings are silvery grey, with a round pale buff blotch of some size occupying the extremity of each wing. The under wings are of the palest buff. The moth rarely flies by day, and may be seen in June and July. At rest the wings are folded round the body, giving the moth rather the appearance of a broken dried twig.

The Cinnabar Moth. Can be seen in May and June. Forewings are greenish black, with a long thin vermillion line running from the body to the wing extremity, and two spots of the same colour on the outer edges of the wing. The hind wings are clear vermillion. Altogether very distinctive and handsome. The caterpillars are an orange yellow with frequent black rings. The insect measures roughly one and a half inches across.

The Common Yellow Underwing. Another very common moth. The forewings may vary from pale to deep brown, mottled with dark brown, usually bearing a single still darker brown spot. The yellow hind wings have a broad but varied band of deep brown and black. Can be seen from June to October.

The Red Underwing. Greyish-brown forewings, covered by a number of wavy irregular lines of a darker grey. Hind wings red with a broad margin of dark grey— almost black—and a central black band terminating half- way down the wing of the same colour. Flies in August and September, and may be found on tree trunks and similar positions.

Section 25

INSECTS

Insects are the most numerous of all living creatures, and in the summer they abound in every place. It is of course quite impossible to do more than describe a few typical specimens. The term insect has been used in its widest sense, to include all those complicated forms of animal life not dealt with under any other heading. Perhaps you are of a scientific turn of mind, and will feel compelled to point out that some of these creatures are not strictly insects; restrain the impulse, because they are insects to us, until we know more of them and their habits. Later, if we are interested, they can be classified scientifically, but for the moment let us have the pleasure of observing them, and the methods they employ in a mighty struggle for existence.

It will be interesting perhaps to note some points of difference between insects and other creatures. The former are covered by a tough skin, which in some cases becomes armour. They do not have rich red blood in veins like the rest of the animal family, but are furnished with colourless or yellow blood, which is dispersed over the body. A still more curious fact is that they are without bones, and therefore have no supporting framework of bones or skeleton.

Beetles

The Dor Beetle. In October the hum of the dor beetle in flight may be heard at dusk. It hides in the ground by day, but owing to its clumsy flight falls an easy prey to owls and other foragers in the evening. The beetle is violet blue in colour, with a smooth shoulder piece, and short, oval, ridged body, unfortunately sometimes covered with parasites. It is one of the last to disappear in autumn, but reappears early in spring.

The Stag Beetle. Seen between June and August buzzing harmlessly at night with laboured flight to feed on the juices of trees. Only the male carries the huge antler-like jaws, which it uses effectively in combat with others of its kind. It has a brownish-purple back, and the wing cases conceal a pair of long shapely wings. The largest of our beetles, it grows to a length of between two and three inches. The caterpillars live in the rotten bark of oaks and similar trees, taking five years to mature.

The Bronze Ground Beetle. Has a bronze iridescent sheen on its long oval body. Carnivorous, and eats all kinds of insects.

The Violet Ground Beetle. Has a long oval body of the same shape as its bronze relative above, but is violet in colour. It runs with great swiftness and hides quickly on being alarmed. Feeds on grubs and wireworms, and sometimes exhibits astonishing fury when attacking its prey.

Two-Barred Wood Beetle. Usually found in pine woods under fallen trees, in which it burrows. It has smooth black wing cases with slanting lines of dull yellow across them. The long thin horns are usually carried at right angles to the head.

The Devil's Coach Horse. Is a great friend of man, as it devours large numbers of insect pests. It is dead black, has a forbidding appearance, and when alarmed cocks its tail over its back in a most startling manner, although quite harmless. The beetle is a vigorous flyer, and has ample wings which are usually folded up under the wing cases.

The Common Burying Beetle. Has a black body barred with orange, and carries a strong smell of musk. Found in the vicinity of some small dead animal, which is scented from afar. The ground underneath is scraped away until the body of the animal sinks down, to be afterwards covered with earth. The eggs are laid inside the carcase, and the grubs subsequently feed on the carrion. To be seen in early spring.

The Bleeding Beetle. Easily recognised by small almost round body, which exudes an unpleasant oily fluid at its joints if touched. The beetle is without wings, and very slow in its movements.

The Tiger Beetle. Plentiful in summer in fields and commons. About three-quarters of an inch in length, of greenish colour with a copper tinge, and five yellow spots. It has long slender legs and is a very fast runner, but on being alarmed will fly. It feeds on wireworms and miscellaneous insects.

Spiders

The Garden Spider. Is dark brown, marked with yellow, the female being much larger than the male, which she often eats. Observe the strength of each strand of the web; neither the wind nor the weight of dew on an autumn morning will destroy it. The threads which go round and round are covered with a sticky substance, but those which radiate from the centre are free. It is the latter which the spider uses to go backwards and forwards. The webs are certainly beautiful, but display many irregularities, and are not the marvels of geometrical symmetry described by some. Watch the web, and you are almost certain to see some unfortunate fly trapped. Unsuspectingly it alights and is pounced on and killed in a moment. The spider may suck its blood, but if not hungry it will envelop its prey in an unbreakable thread and suspend it for some unsavoury feast later. Spiders will only feed on insects which they have killed themselves.

The Funnel-Web Spider. Towards autumn you will find in the hedges tangles of strong compact web, from one part of which a sort of funnel runs down at a slant. It is wide at the top but narrows to a small tube, and contains the spider, which is brown with a herring-bone mark on its back.

Shade-Loving Spider. Is large, of a dark brown colour, with a flattish body and six to eight small depressions down its back. It prefers darkness and is seldom seen in daylight. Frequents crannies in walls, and is also found under the bark of dead trees. When alarmed it feigns death, and although evil-looking is quite incapable of doing harm.

The Wolf Spider. Several species will be found in May and June, running swiftly among dead leaves in or near woods on a sunny day. It is dark and hairy in appearance, with eight long legs. The males have a white-striped thorax, which is missing in the female; the latter has a habit of rolling herself up when alarmed, hoping to escape unnoticed. The males disappear in the autumn, but the female carries her eggs about in a little bag. At a later stage this bursts, and the young emerge and cling to the mother, who carries them with her. The wolf spider hunts and catches its prey, and does not use a web.

The Cockchafer. Plentiful on a warm summer evening. It is about half an inch long. The body, ending in a point or tail, is brown, and the wing cases are of the same colour, slightly ridged. The shoulder piece is smooth, and on the extremity of its feelers are little feathery appendages, which are much larger in the male than in the female. The grub is an unpleasant-looking creature of a dirty yellow colour, and resembles a big hairless caterpillar. It is found in the ground, where it remains for nearly four years, doing an immense amount of damage to crops in the meantime.

The Glow Worm. The grub is little over a quarter of an inch in length, and except for being slightly larger, the female differs very little from the grub; both have their bodies divided up into well-defined sections, have six legs and tiny horns or feelers on the head. The female gives a brilliant and persistent pale greenish light at night. The male is a little flying beetle of a dull black colour. These creatures feed primarily on snails, and are therefore useful in keeping down pests.

The Dragonfly. The hot sunny days of July and August are the dragonfly seasons. It is one of the most noticeable of our insects, and yet one of the most elusive. It frequents ponds and streamsides for food, but may be found flying at great speed far afield. The large powerful wings, generally iridescent, show a clear division between the front and hind pair. About thirty different kinds exist in England, and they vary greatly in size. The long slender body is magnificently coloured, being bright metallic blue, green or copper. Although feared by many, possibly because of its massive head, the dragonfly is quite innocuous, and feeds on insects and spiders. The larvæ are about two inches long and live an active life in some pond, but when the period of change comes, they climb out on to a reed. It is interesting to note that the chrysalid retains the same shape as the larva.

The Grasshopper. Emerges from the egg in practically the same form as its parents. The most common variety, the small green grasshopper, may be found in every field

11

during the summer, and even if you do not see it at once, you will hear its insistent chirping noise. This is made by rubbing the hind leg against the wing cover. The great green grasshopper is several times the size of his small relative, but is nevertheless quite common. The female possesses a curious long tube at the back, which is inserted into the ground when the eggs are laid. If you examine the powerful, bent, hind legs you will see the explanation of the surprising jumping capabilities of these small creatures.

The Cricket. Four varieties, two of which only will interest us for the moment. The house cricket is usually a resident of the home, as it likes warmth, but in summer may be found sometimes in cracks in the wall and similar sheltered positions. It is heard more often than seen, and makes a persistent chirp by drawing the tooth-like edge of one wing over the other. This is really the call of the male to the female, and the former only are capable of making the sound. It is about an inch long, of a brownish-yellow colour, with long antennæ and legs, somewhat resembling a grasshopper. The female lays eggs, which hatch out into larvæ, carrying antennæ. The larvæ gradually develop a shape very similar to the perfect insect before changing into the chrysalis, which retains the same form.

The field cricket is very similar to its house-loving relative, but is perhaps a little darker in colour, with a conspicuous blackish head. It makes a home in the ground, where the eggs are deposited.

The Crane-fly. Known as the daddy-long-legs, and familiar to all. Has a slender body and six ungainly long brittle legs, which are not infrequently broken off, apparently without great inconvenience to the insect. The wings are narrow and transparent, about the same length as the body, but the insect seems capable of rapid and sustained flight. The female is slightly longer in the body than the male, which is due to the egg tube, which is thrust into the ground to lay large numbers of black eggs. The grubs are over an inch in length, are of a brownish colour, and have tough outer skins from which they derive their name of "leather jackets." These grubs live underground, where by their voracious habits they do an immense amount of harm, and are a pest to farmers.

The Earwig. The idea that the earwig will enter and damage the ear of a sleeping person still persists, but is of course quite incorrect. The antennæ, or feelers, are long, and like other insects, they have six legs. The long pincers at the tail end look very alarming, but beyond a slight nip are incapable of harm. The earwig has wings under its horny back casing, but does not use them to any extent. Eggs are laid, but there is no caterpillar or chrysalis stage, the little light-coloured insects emerging direct from the eggs.

The Centipede. Is universally disliked, but inoffensive. It is about an inch long, and short in comparison with its width. The centipede has less legs than the millipede, as the former possesses one pair to each body segment, and the latter two pairs. It is found under stones and in dark places, and is without sight, or at the best can only distinguish the difference between light and darkness. The absence of sight is compensated by the provision of two very sensitive feelers. Centipedes are flesh eaters, and feed on worms and similar prey; millipedes, however, are vegetarians.

The Great Water Beetle. There can be no mistaking the large oval, inch-long, dark brown body of this pond dweller, which in the case of the male has smooth wing cases and little discs on the front legs covered with some adhesive to enable it to hold on to the female. The latter has grooved wing cases, and is without the leg discs. Although this beetle spends a greater part of its time in the water, it has fore and hind wings, and can fly. The front wings are horny, and enclose a space for storing air, when the creature is under water. If you watch you will see it rise to the surface every few minutes and push its tail above the water. In actual fact it is expelling used air from the wing reservoir, and taking in a fresh supply. The beetle is carnivorous, and feeds on tadpoles, worms and small fish. The eggs are laid on the stalks of water plants, and the larvæ, which grow to two inches in length, are flat-headed and formidable looking; they are more than this, in fact, and are a positive menace to other residents of the pond. They do not actually eat their victims, but suck them dry and will attack even larvæ of their own kind, or, for that matter, the parent beetles. Handle both the larva and beetle with discretion, as both are capable of inflicting a small wound.

The Caddis Fly. Is a moth-like creature with a slender body, transparent wings, and long antennæ. When at rest the wings are folded over the body. The eggs are laid on the water and appear as a lump of jelly. From these the larvæ emerge, which are soft-bodied little worms, having two hooks at the end of their bodies. To protect itself from its many enemies the larva builds itself a small retreat composed of pieces of wood, moss and similar things, cemented together by a glue which comes from the creature's mouth. The worm lives inside this house, from which it sometimes emerges to feed, but more often is fixed by its two hooks. In due course it cements up the open end of its house in preparation for the final change into the perfect insect.

Section 26

REPTILES AND AMPHIBIANS

Snakes

The Adder. Length about twenty inches, and, as it is the only poisonous British snake, it may be justifiably killed; but make quite sure it is an adder before doing so. The definite wavy zig-zag dark mark down the back is an infallible distinguishing mark. The head is flat and broad behind, the tail short and blunt in the male, but long and pointed in the female. It is common on moors and heaths, but less frequent in woods and coppices.

The adder does not sting, as many suppose, and its forked shooting tongue is harmless. The real danger lies in a bite from the two long sharp pointed teeth in the upper jaw. The maximum distance at which the snake can reach you is half its own length. The wound shows two small round punctures. It is followed by great local pain and swelling, and in bad cases delirium. Vomiting may set in, breathing will be difficult, and the voice may lose its power. These symptoms may last for some hours, but, in the ordinary run of events, then subside.

If bitten, first enlarge the wound by making a criss-cross with a sharp knife, suck the wound hard and spit out the poison; if there is no broken skin in the mouth the operation is harmless. If the wound is on a limb, tie a ligature above. Apply permanganate of potash crystals if available, or burn the surface with a piece of red-hot wire.

On being alarmed, the adder will glide swiftly into cover. It is by no means fierce, and will not attack man unless unable to escape or trodden on. The food consists of field mice, voles and young birds. The eggs are not laid, but are hatched out inside the adder, and this gives rise to the popular fallacy that the female swallows her young for safety.

The Grass Snake. Is olive green, with several rows of black spots running the entire length of the back. It also has a pale yellow mark, like a collar, on each side of the neck, and is longer than an adder. The food consists almost entirely of frogs and newts, and it is therefore found more frequently in damp localities. Unlike the adder, it lays eggs, and is quite harmless. Do not kill it, even if it does look threatening.

The Slow Worm, or Blind Worm. Has no scale or line down its back. It is shiny and small, rarely exceeding twelve inches in length, and is not really a snake but a legless lizard. The little creature is fairly common, and may be found under old tree trunks or similar cover. On discovery it remains perfectly motionless, but will slip rapidly into the herbage if you attempt a capture. It is harmless, and in addition useful to man, as slugs are its staple diet. If seized it can divest itself of part of its tail without harm.

The Sand Lizard. Is a sandy brown colour, tinged with green and marked with blackish brown and white. The body is about three inches long and the tail of similar length. It is fairly common in certain localities and may be found on sunny banks basking in the sunshine. Feeds on all small insects, which it seizes in its jaws and kills, afterwards chewing them before swallowing. The sand lizard produces young from eggs. It is incapable of doing any damage, and is easily caught.

The Common Lizard. Britain's smallest reptile. Numerous in the south of England, where they may be found sunning themselves on bare patches on banks in mid-July. They are brown in colour, and this gives them an admirable protection in their natural surroundings.

The snout is more pointed than that of the sand lizard. Feeds on insects. Possesses the same curious feature as the slow worm, and, if seized by the tail, will break off that member and escape, afterwards growing a new tail. Hibernates during winter.

The Frog. The frog lays its eggs in the water in the form of tiny black specks coated with jelly. These soon swell to the size of a pea, with the black dot in the centre. Frogs' eggs adhere together in numbers, forming a large jelly-like mass, to be found in ponds in spring. In course of time the familiar tadpoles emerge, and while in this state breathe through gills like fish. However, they feed greedily and develop rapidly; legs appear and gills close up. At this stage the youngster comes to the surface frequently for air, and finally settles himself on a piece of weed. Now the last stage of the transformation starts, and the tail is absorbed into the body, and the complete frog is ready to move. He now feeds on insects instead of weeds, and catches them by means of a sticky tongue. Lives on land during summer, but hibernates in mud during winter.

Frogs are smooth, rather brightly coloured, with a dark stripe from the eye down to the side of the throat, but undoubtedly vary their colour according to their surroundings. They are alert-looking creatures, and leap by means of long, powerful, hind legs.

The Toad. Often mistaken for a frog, but quite different, as it has a rough skin and is dull in colour. It is fat, sits lazily, and when on the move usually crawls, although it can jump. Lays eggs much in the same way as the frog, but where the former's eggs are in the mass, those of the toad are connected rather in the form of a long string of jelly-like peas. A friend of man and harmless, although unpopular because of its appearance. Eats slugs, grubs and insects. The skin secretes an acid which is sufficiently unpleasant to prevent interference from dogs, although some do kill toads. Casts its skin and eats it.

Great Water Newt. Can be distinguished from lizards by their flat tail and amphibian habits. They are hatched out as tadpoles in much the same way as frogs and toads. About six inches from nose to end of tail. In the breeding season, up to July, the male is very beautiful, having a green back and orange under side. The back is decorated with a wavy crest, giving the general appearance of some miniature prehistoric animal. They spend about nine months of the year on land, but take to the water during breeding season.

Common Newt. Smaller than the great newt, and brown in colour. It exhibits the same habits as its bigger cousin, and spends the greater part of its time on land, returning to the water for breeding purposes only.

Chapter V

SECRETS OF THE COUNTRYSIDE

Section 27

A COUNTRY DIARY MONTH BY MONTH

Here is a diary of some common objects to be observed throughout the year. It is not comprehensive or systematic, but rather the jottings of years of observation. Start making a nature diary for yourself by taking notes on your walks. Be patient, and when the long winter evenings come, write it up fully.

A COUNTRY DIARY MONTH BY MONTH

January

The holly is now at its best, and the bright red berries provide a welcome touch of colour in a sombre countryside. Note the prickles on the lower leaves are a measure of protection from being eaten by animals. The higher leaves are devoid of this protection.

Mistletoe berries are still plentiful, and it is interesting to observe that they will not actually ripen until March.

The snowdrop has made its welcome appearance as a harbinger of brighter days. Winter has not yet passed, but its end is heralded.

Here and there you will find solitary dandelions and daisies exhibiting their flowers, almost as a challenge to any heavy weather ahead.

In this lean month make a list of flowers having the courage to bloom. Among them you will find the common groundsel, which flowers all the year round, the white deadnettle, the red deadnettle, shepherd's purse and chickweed. If the weather is not too severe you may discover the first primrose.

Lambs are born about this time.

The tortoiseshell butterfly, which has been hibernating in some warm corner during the winter, is now on the move. Occasional cabbage white butterflies may also be noticed.

If you see moths, they will probably be males of the pale brindled beauty or the spring usher. Both have wingless females.

This is the month to learn the song of our hardy winter birds before it is drowned in the great spring chorus. The skylark, song-thrush, blackbird, common bunting, robin, nuthatch and wren may all be heard occasionally. Try and memorise their songs. House-sparrows begin chirping, and chaffinches begin to mate. Starlings begin to build their nests.

If the days are sunny, hares will commence their love-making. Watch one feeding, and if you are lucky you will see him suddenly spring into the air and then resume feeding; a second spring and perhaps a third, and then, forced by some unaccountable impulse, he will run away for about a hundred yards, and then just as suddenly resume his feeding.

The first house-flies are to be seen—the advance guard of a villainous army.

Snails awakened from their winter sleep may be seen on the move.

Watch some of the beautiful effects of frost, and if you are a photographer you will get some good pictures.

The hazel is the very earliest of our British trees to bloom, and already you will find the nutbushes decorated with male catkins, which grow longer with each mild day. As yet, however, they are smooth and hard.

February

Pond life becomes more active. The common newt can be discovered by a careful search, and the first water boatmen appear. They are curious creatures, with a pair of middle legs fashioned and used like oars. Frog spawn is in the ponds and ditches. You cannot mistake the mass of jelly, many times the size of a frog. Look at it closely, and you will find each transparent egg larger than a threepenny piece, with a small black spot in the centre. When the egg is laid, it is only a little larger than the black spot; subsequently the water soaks in through the outer skin of the egg, and it swells. By next month you will find the small black spot has developed into a tadpole.

The sallow may now be observed. This is the yellow palm so much sought for at Easter. The silken catkins are arranged tightly on the branches, but later they will push themselves out to flowering length in time for Palm Sunday.

Hazel catkins have become loose and show the small yellow male flower.

The male catkins of the alder are growing longer, and appear before the leaves. Examine a branch carefully. You will see in addition to the male catkin the small egg-shaped catkin of the female flower, and very often the skeletons of last year's catkins.

The yew is now interesting. Its male flowers are in short catkins and are highly poisonous. The female flowers stand erect in small cup-shaped discs, which when fertilised develop into beautiful red berries. These, by the way, are not poisonous, although I cannot recommend them. The leaves of the yew often prove fatal to cattle.

Rooks are busy with their nests. The leaves have not yet appeared on their tree homes to obscure their movements, and an amusing half-hour may be spent watching them, particularly if you have field-glasses.

The brown owl hoots in the woods, and you will hear the coo of the woodpigeon. Blue tits will be heard chirping, and the cry of the green woodpecker is noticeable. The goldfinch and greenfinch both start singing. This is the time to observe the tree creeper to advantage, as he searches crevices in the bark for food. Note how he seems to glide up the tree and to pursue a twisting course round the trunk. He is one of our smallest birds.

The shooting season is over, and partridges begin to pair and coveys break up into separate households. Take care not to disturb them.

An occasional bluebottle staggers on the warm window-sill. He drags his legs wearily, and is hungry after a long winter in some obscure corner. He must be wary, or he will fall an easy victim to enterprising birds. How unlike the desperado who drives us frantic later in the year with his interminable buzz! Gnats put in an appearance, and the first cricket is seen.

The first white violets may be found in the hedgerows, and the early daffodils are opening up. The yellow flowers of the coltsfoot appear before the downy leaves; later the flower will be replaced by a bunch of white fluffy seeds. In the woods the dainty purple-blue blossoms of the lesser periwinkle stand up on the trailing stem of the plant. The butcher's broom is curious and easy to identify, as the small greenish-yellow flowers seem to spring from the middle of its leaves. These flowers are succeeded later by rather striking red berries.

The pale blue flowers of the ivy-leaved speedwell depend on mild weather, and the same may be said of the lesser celandine, which will put on its first golden blooms on some favourable bank.

The yellow furze is commencing its annual transformation of the countryside.

Primroses are more plentiful. They are distasteful to animals to eat, and their extermination is therefore due to human agency. Treat them kindly.

The brimstone butterfly is now on the wing. You cannot mistake his wonderful deep yellow appearance, far deeper in colour than the creamy yellow of the so-called whites.

March

The eggs of the toad can now be found. In size and shape they are similar to those of the frog, but are laid in long jelly-like strings instead of in the mass.

The hedgehog will make his first venture into the open. He will still be a little shy and uncertain of his plans, and will retire again into his winter retreat at the first sign of frost.

In the woods and hedgerows the wild arum or cuckoo-pint has sent up its glossy deep green leaves, shaped something like a spear head. Many of these leaves exhibit curious blotches or black spots.

The early daisies have now been followed by myriads of their brethren. You may notice that the later flowers are pink tipped, while those of January and February have pure white petals.

The bluebell, or wild hyacinth, carpets the woods, but can only remain there if indiscriminate picking is sternly discouraged.

The pinky-white flowers of lady's smock are abundant.

They grow in clusters at the top of the stalk. This plant is sometimes called the cuckoo-flower, because it blooms at the same time as the first cuckoo is heard.

The funnel-shaped flowers of the cowslip grow in a cluster at the end of a long stalk. They are a rich deep yellow, easily distinguishable from the pale yellow of the primrose.

The bluish-purple blossoms of the ground ivy carpet the rough dry ground. It can be identified by its rough kidney-shaped leaves.

Moorhens begin to pair, and the magpie builds its nest. The nest of the song-thrush may be found in some sheltered niche. You may notice that it dispenses with the inner lining of grass used by its friends the missel-thrush and blackbird. You cannot fail to find the nest of the missel-thrush, which builds long before the leaves are out. The big untidy nests, containing four or five greenish-brown spotted eggs, are usually placed between the fork of two branches. The robin usually chooses a sheltered spot for a nesting site. Its loosely constructed nest of moss and leaves can be found in a hole in the bank, or in some old pot or tin can. The eggs are cream-coloured streaked with reddish brown, and usually number about five.

The hedgerows are brightened by the delicate blossom of the sloe or blackthorn, which covers the dark thorny twigs before many leaves have been unfurled. The white-thorn or hawthorn, on the other hand, leafs before flowering. This is an example of the abundance of blossom on the early flowering trees, and is nature's precaution against the many risks run at this season.

Ivy berries are blackening and ripening.

Leaves break on the dog-rose, horse-chestnut, crab-apple, alder tree, birch and lime.

Elm trees are now throwing out their tiny reddish flowers. It is difficult to distinguish the colour at a distance, but you will notice that the delicate tracery of the twigs will not be so sharply defined as it was in the autumn.

It is early blossom time, and you will see the wild pear, modest in height, but with large white flowers. The fruit is hard and useless. The wild cherry is somewhat larger in stature when well grown, but its flowers are also white. The wild plum exhibits white flowers, but the tree is usually found in hedges and rarely exceeds twenty feet in height.

Ants are to be seen for the first time, and the earwig makes a sluggish entry into spring.

The peacock butterfly with the wonderful eye markings on its four purple wings can be seen in fields and lanes.

The March moth is on the wing, but its neutral greyish colour will make it difficult to detect. As with nearly all the early moths, the female is wingless, and therefore able to hide herself from the many dangers which beset her kind at this time of the year.

April

The orange tip butterfly is now on the wing. At a distance he can easily be mistaken for one of the common whites, but if you get closer you will discover a wide difference. The male orange tip is distinguished from the female by a broad splash of orange at the tip of each wing. In the female this is replaced by a splash of greyish black. The under sides of both sexes are a beautiful mottled green.

The butter-bur is one of the earliest of our nectar-producing plants. You will find it by the edge of streams and in damp places. The purple blossoms fade and fall before the leaves appear. These leaves are remarkable for their size—indeed, they are some of the largest of our British plants.

The larches now bear their soft purple cone-like flowers. To distinguish a larch from a spruce or pine, remember that the larch loses its leaves in winter.

The yellow flowers of the common broom now make a brave display on a bush which sometimes grows six feet high.

The small white flowers of the wild chervil, growing in clusters on furrowed stems, are common in spring. Another name for this plant is beaked parsley, and this gives the clue to the shape of the leaf. In bogs and streams the marsh marigold or kingcup displays itself in glorious golden patches. The wood anemone is one of the most delightful of our wild flowers. The white blooms tinged with pink can be found both in woods and fields. The leaves open after the flowers have appeared. The water crowfoot, or water buttercup, is white with a yellowish centre. It has now commenced to bloom, and by the end of the month will be covering the surface of some pools with a sheet of white. Some of the leaves float on the surface, while others exist quite submerged. In moist and shady hedgerows the graceful wood sorrel exhibits its little white flowers among three-lobed clover-like leaves.

The lime tree is bursting into leaf.

The purple bluish flowers of the dog violet are larger than those of the sweet violet. It is found on heaths and dry hillsides, and is without scent.

The little white blossoms of the wild strawberry are coming out, and will be succeeded later by the miniature well-flavoured fruit.

The swallows arrive about April 13th, and a few days later the house martins follow.

The cup-shaped nest of the linnet may now be found in low bushes, on gorse, and even in the hedge. It is simple in structure, and made of small twigs and dry grass with a lining of down. The linnet lays five or six eggs of a bluish-white colour spotted with deep brown. Occasionally a number of nests will be found quite near each other.

The moorhen will have laid about nine eggs of a buff colour speckled with deep brown. You will find its nest among the reeds at the water edge—a rough-looking piece of work composed of reeds, and lined with leaves and fine grass.

The nightingale and cuckoo can be heard.

The thrush is now having a good time with an unending diet of snails. He will carry each capture to a favourite stone, where he beats it until the shell breaks. Having swallowed the tasty morsel, he will go off and fetch another, and continue this operation until his appetite is satisfied. In course of time the stone becomes surrounded by broken shells, and is known as a "thrush's breakfast table."

Towards the end of the month, some early hatched young thrushes may be found in the nest.

The blackbird lays on an average five sea-green eggs flecked with cinnamon. His nest is similar to that of the thrush, but you may distinguish it by the final lining of dry grass.

You may hear the harsh note of the jay, and will be rewarded for a patient wait if you see the bird itself. It travels with a dipping sort of flight, but the plumage of blue, shading into almost every tint of purple and grey, renders it unmistakable.

12

Tadpoles are seen in the ponds.

Single jelly-like eggs of the newt may now be found wrapped in the leaves of water plants. When the tadpoles emerge, it will be observed that, unlike frogs and toads, they have external gills.

May

The hawthorn, whitethorn or may is now in flower, and its somewhat overpowering smell is familiar to all. Jack-by-the-hedge may be found in the fields and in the hedgerow. It has small white flowers, and possesses an unpleasant smell like garlic. The bogbean or buckbean is most attractive. Its white flowers, tinged with red, are covered with lace-like threads and have a background of rich green trefoil leaves. Found usually in boggy land. Another inhabitant of damp places is the ragged robin, which has rose-coloured petals surmounting a deeper red calyx. The plant grows to a height of about two feet, and the stem is of a reddish colour. The charlock or wild mustard is much in evidence, and although good to look at, is a pest to farmers. It has bright yellow flowers and very rough leaves, with tooth-like edges. The flowers of the yarrow vary in colour from white to pink, and grow in clusters at the top of the stems. The leaves, which grow direct from the stems, are divided into little feathery sections. The plant has a very pleasant smell and flourishes everywhere. The stitchwort has white star-like flowers, and narrow leaves almost like grass. It fights for existence in the crowded hedge, and its long, slender, brittle stems struggle through much stronger competitors. The leaves of the fumitory are graceful and fernlike, and the small flowers are rose coloured, tipped with crimson. It is usually found in dry fields and similar situations.

The buds of the wild crab-apple are now conspicuous, the blossom red without and pinkish white within. The flower spikes of the horse-chestnut are growing, and the flowers are at their best about the middle of May. This tree is one of the first to burst into leaf, and its fruits are the familiar "conkers."

Both red and white clovers are in flower.

The skylark builds in the open fields of grass or corn, and thereby escapes many of the dangers which exist in the hedgerow. The nest is difficult to find, owing to the bird's habit of alighting some distance from the nest and running along the ground, obscured by the tall grasses. Four or five eggs are laid of a pale green colour, spotted with deep brown.

The nest of the nightingale is usually found on the ground in a wooded locality. Four or five olive-coloured eggs rest in a loosely made nest of grass and dead leaves.

The greenfinch is not particular in choosing a site for its nest, which has an untidy exterior but a good lining of moss, feathers and even hair. The eggs are of the palest blue, spotted with deep brown, and number four or five.

The bullfinch builds in a high hedge or thick bushes some four feet from the ground. Its nest is neater than that of the greenfinch, and can be distinguished by the fact that the tiny cup-like structure is placed on a platform of twigs. The eggs are a deeper blue than the greenfinch's and more distinctly spotted.

The nest of the yellowhammer may be found in gorse or thorn bushes, on commons, or by the roadside. It lays four to five grey eggs with veinings of deep purplish red.

Many young birds may be seen about this time. It is often difficult to identify them, but if you watch quietly the parent bird in the vicinity will give you the clue.

The first dragonflies are on the wing.

The beetle family are becoming more active, and among the many to be seen the violet ground beetle will be the most handsome. He is carnivorous, and lives on smaller living creatures, such as caterpillars.

The white ermine moth makes its appearance. The name is most descriptive and makes identification easy.

The brimstone moth is seen. It is pale yellow in colour, with two well-defined brown triangles on the front edge of its wings.

The lime hawk emerges from its chrysalis this month, and may be found on the trunks of lime trees about shoulder high from the ground. It should be easy to recognise, as it has beautifully scalloped wings marked with olive green and brown.

The small heath butterfly is about in large numbers. Note when he settles that the grey under sides of his wings only are to be seen, and he becomes almost invisible.

June

The nightingale has ceased to sing until next spring, although he may still be heard croaking in the woods.

You will notice that the bird chorus is gradually ceasing.

Young robins and sparrows are adventuring alone, as their parents are now preoccupied with their second sets of eggs. Young linnets are numerous in the gorse.

The slow worm, or blind worm, may be seen. It is not necessary to kill them, as they are really legless lizards, and quite harmless. Notice the skin, which is quite shiny and without the scales of the snake. Most important of all, there is no wavy line down the back which indicates the adder and danger.

At this time of the year you cannot fail to notice small accumulations of white froth on some plants. This is known widely as cuckoo-spit, but is really the frothy secretion of the frog-hopper, a little brown insect which skips amazing distances. If you rub aside the froth you will see the yellow, immature insect.

The cow-parsnip is a conspicuous object in the countryside, as it often grows five or six feet high. It has a thick, rough, grooved, hollow stem, branching at the top into clusters of white flowers. The dry stems often remain during the winter, and give comfortable quarters to beetles and other small creatures.

The sow-thistle, growing two or three feet high, stands out among the herbage. The flowers are yellow and produce small fluffy seedballs to be carried away by the wind. This plant is sometimes called the milk thistle, because of the milky juice in its stems.

The bittersweet, or woody nightshade, is in flower in the hedges. It is a trailing climber with small clusters of dark purple flowers, each with a yellow spike in the middle. Unlike the deadly nightshade, the bunches of deep red berries are not poisonous, although not recommended to be eaten. The deadly nightshade produces large black berries, something like cherries.

In the pastures and hay fields the ox-eye daisies show in great patches of dazzling white.

Watercress is in bloom. Its small flowers may be either white or yellow.

The willow-herb, or fireweed, seems to be increasing, and great masses of tall pink flower spikes form a bright border to many woods and copses. The feathery seeds are carried about in large numbers by the wind.

You will have no difficulty in identifying the great mullein. It has large woolly leaves growing near the ground, and a woolly stem four to six feet high, bearing a solid spike of small yellow flowers.

The bladder campion may be noticed by the roadside.

It is a peculiar plant, as the calyx, or exterior covering of the flower, has the appearance of a small inflated bladder, out of the top of which project the creamy white petals.

The familiar honeysuckle is decorating the hedge, and attracting large numbers of bees to its well-filled flowers.

Marshy lands are now brightened by the purple blue flowers of the meadow cranesbill, which is the largest British geranium.

The flowers of the wild rose, ranging in colour from white to deep pink, hang in festoons from the hedges.

The pale lilac flower of the scabious adds its share to the galaxy of colour in the pasture land. It will fall a victim to the haycutter at any moment now.

Tadpoles begin to develop their legs.

Wasps are about in great numbers.

The buff tip moth is exceedingly well protected by natural colouring, and is difficult to notice when resting on the bark of a tree with its wings folded over its body It is silver grey in colour, like the bark of a dead twig. At the end of each wing is a buff circle surrounded by a thin double brown line, resembling exactly the broken end of a dry twig. When the upper wings are opened for flight, it will be observed that the under wings, invisible at rest, are a pale buff colour.

The common tiger moth is one of the most handsome of all British moths. Its upper wings are a deep chocolate, streaked with cream, and its under wings are scarlet with black circles. Its caterpillar is the well-known woolly bear, and is covered with long silky hair, black beneath and silver grey on top.

The red admiral butterfly is to be seen on the stinging nettles. The front wings are deep brown with a red bar dividing the brown from the black wing tips, which are spotted with white. The rear wings are brown, with a broad red margin.

The buzz of the grasshopper may now be heard.

Only the male stag beetle carries antlers, and although he looks alarming, he is quite harmless. This beetle may be seen in the late evening, flying clumsily between the trees from which he sucks the juices.

July

Fallow deer are about with new-born fawns.

The hedgehog may be found by the roadside in the evening on some foraging expedition. At home he will have a family covered with soft white spines, which are Nature's provision to enable the mother to attend to her babies without the inconvenience which would accompany the sharp spines which develop later.

Young magpies are in the woods. They are handsome birds, and can be distinguished at a distance by their black and white colour and long tails.

Young jays are much in evidence. Owing to their more fluffy plumage, they look larger than their parents.

Young green woodpeckers can be seen on the tree trunks, which they climb actively as soon as they leave the nest. They are a duller green than their parents, and have black-and-white heads.

Young greenfinch families chatter ceaselessly.

The hemlock is chiefly noticeable by its peculiar mousy smell. The plant is tall and grows up to six feet. It has large fern-like leaves, and the flat heads of small white flowers form on its many branches at the top of a smooth spotted stem.

The blackberry or bramble is in flower everywhere.

The wild chicory opens its wide pale blue flowers, which are attached to the stem without stalks. The leaves resemble those of the dandelion, and the root when dried and ground is mixed with coffee.

Ragwort is pleasing to the eye, but a nuisance to farmers. It grows about three to four feet high, and is crowned with a large number of daisy-like yellow flowers. When bruised it gives out an unpleasant smell.

The mallow produces large lilac flowers darkening to the centre. It grows to a height of three or four feet on a hairy stem. The seed vessels, from their shape, are sometimes called "cheeses."

In pasture land the dwarf plume thistle is numerous and unmistakable. Its spiny leaves form a rosette on the ground, in the centre of which a stemless crimson thistle head appears.

Poppies are now providing great scarlet patches in the landscape, and the bright blue cornflower is in the cornfields. Another treasure to be found in and around the cornfields is the corncockle, which grows to a height of about four feet. The large crimson-purple blossoms are at the top of heavy stems, and the leaves are long and narrow, similar to the leaves of the neighbouring corn plants.

The pale greenish yellow flower of the male wild hop is in the hedgerow.

If your route is along the road, you will find the grass verges brightened by the golden yellow of agrimony. The flowers are like little yellow roses attached to a central stem by short stalks. They have a smell not unlike apricots, but curiously enough do not contain honey, and are therefore seldom visited by bees or other insects. The fruits which form later are little burrs, which will cling firmly to your stockings.

By the side of shallow streams you may see billowy masses of creamy white flowers. Individually they are minute, but combined on the top of the stems they appear as dense masses of flower with a most pleasing smell. This is the meadowsweet, one of our most graceful water-side plants.

The wheat harvest begins.

Young frogs appear on land.

The eggs of the snail may be found under fallen leaves. They are clusters of semi-transparent soft eggs, like little pills.

On woodland paths and damp places huge black slugs can be observed. They are arion slugs, and often grow four inches in length. Touch one and see how he shrinks under the shield on top of his body. This shield protects all vital parts.

The common lizard is much in evidence at this time, basking on sunny banks. He moves over the ground quite slowly, and is easily caught, although his sudden movements give an impression of speed.

At this time of the year you may find clusters of small mottled yellowish caterpillars on the under sides of half-eaten leaves of the lime, poplar and similar trees. These will probably be the caterpillar of the buff tip moth. They soon reach full growth and are then large and fat, variegated with yellow and black, but not hairy.

The ringlet butterfly is flying in shady lanes. It is interesting from the fact that the upper sides of the wings of deep brown have scarcely any marking, but underneath the golden brown colour is decorated eight perfect little rings on each side.

The swallow tail moth has rather large pale yellow wings, and is very conspicuous in the lanes at night. When at rest you will notice the pointed extremities of its under wings.

The ghost moth is seen on the wing in grassy places.

The male has long silvery white wings and a dark body. He hovers in the air as though suspended by some invisible thread, but if alarmed will disappear suddenly by dropping to the ground.

The yellow underwing is one of the most abundant of all British moths, and may be found everywhere. It has upper wings of varied shades of brown, and lower wings of deep yellow with a broad black band round the edges. When at rest the lower wings are covered, and it is difficult to observe.

Soldier beetles may be seen scrambling over the flowers. They are long and thin in shape and dull red in colour.

August

Most of the young starlings have now collected into flocks, and later these flocks will combine into the vast hordes which are so entertaining to watch in flight during the autumn. The soft brown plumage of the young starling is in contrast to the glossy spangled feathers of his parents.

The yellowhammer, linnet and goldfinch cease singing about this time, leaving practically only the skylark, greenfinch and chiff-chaff still giving us their music.

Frogs and toads are abundant at this time of the year. As many people confuse them, here is the broad difference. The toad is rough skinned and dull in colour; the frog is smooth and rather brightly coloured, with a dark stripe from the eye down the side of the throat. The frog has longer hind legs and sits in an alert position. The toad, on the other hand, has a fat body and sits lazily with its legs tucked under it. The frog leaps more than the toad; the latter usually crawls, but can jump if it wishes.

You may come across an adder in your rambles, and it is important to be able to recognise the only venomous reptile in Britain. This is not difficult if you remember that the adder has a most distinct zig-zag black marking down the whole length of its back.

The bush vetch is found principally in the hedges, scrambling over other plants, often to a considerable height. It has clusters of dark purple pea-like flowers, which are succeeded later by smooth black seed pods.

The great bindweed, or convolvulus, grows unrestrained at this time of the year. Its beautiful large white bell flowers are too well known to need description.

The handsome purple flower of the black knapweed is at its best. It somewhat resembles a thistle flower, but is not prickly. The seeds are formed in little solid knobs at the end of stiff stalks.

The common teasel is one of the most striking of British wild plants, as a well-grown specimen reaches between five and six feet in height. It has stout, angular, spiny stems, crowned by the prickly cylindrical heads of purple flowers.

Travellers' joy, or wild clematis, flourishes best in chalky districts. It is a common hedge shrub, and a good climber, often occupying more than its fair share of the space. It has small clusters of white flowers, which possess a strong but pleasant smell. Later these develop into conspicuous tufts of feathery seeds, known as "Old Man's Beard."

The heather, or ling, is now spreading its purple colouring over the moorland. The magenta variety, which has been in flower for some time, is bell heather.

Examples of the spear plume thistle are found everywhere. It varies greatly in size, but occasionally reaches feet, with purple flower heads often an inch in length.

Its long lance-shaped leaves are deeply cut and protected by long sharp spikes.

The barley crop is being cut.

The horse mushroom is now found. It is similar in everything but size to the ordinary mushroom, and often measures six inches across. It is edible for those who care to attempt it, but tough and not much favoured.

By the water, the great reed mace is now prominent. It is commonly known as the bulrush.

The nest of the wood wasp is made from wood pulp, and is about the size of a large orange. It may be seen this time of the year hanging from a tree branch.

It is possible that you may find some luckless caterpillar growing limp and flabby with a strange silk growth spread out on either side of it. This is the work of the small ichneumon fly, which feeds on caterpillars and restricts many pests, particularly the white cabbage butterfly.

The old lady moth is out in August. Both upper and lower wings are of a dingy brown colour, measuring about three inches across.

The red underwing moth is another example of protective colouring, as when it is resting on a tree trunk, the upper neutral-coloured wings make it almost invisible. Disturb it, and you will see a flash of bright crimson as the under wings are revealed with a broad band of black on their edges. The appearance of the red underwing is a sign of shortening days.

The magpie or currant moth is well known, as it is abundant everywhere. The wings are creamy white, with a yellow streak near the body and towards the edge of the upper wings, which bear in addition five or six rows of black spots. The under wings have two rows of black spots, and the body is yellow and also bears a line black spots. There are innumerable varieties of this marking.

September

The flat loose clusters of berries of the dogwood are to be seen in the hedge. The pointed oval leaves, which are green in summer, have now darkened to purple, and the stalks are the same colour. This renders recognition easy.

The devil's-bit scabious may still be seen in meadows and pastures. It is a slender plant with purplish-blue flowers.

In marsh land the grass of Parnassus can be found. The name is misleading, as it is not a grass at all, but has heart-shaped leaves on long stalks. The flowers are veined and white, carried singly on upright stems. The plant was known in ancient Greece.

The blackberry crop can now be gathered, as the hedges will be hanging heavily with deep red and purple berries.

Hazel nuts are to be seen in plenty—they are ripe and ready for picking.

The milk thistle is easily recognised by its beautiful green leaves, webbed heavily with white.

The green shells of the horse-chestnut fall, and when they have burst, disclose the ripe nuts or "conkers."

Walnuts are now ready for gathering. Remember that those green shells will stain your hands an unpleasant brown. Rooks are particularly fond of walnuts, and will strip a tree in an incredibly short time.

The dying leaves of the sycamore now begin to fall.

This is mushroom time, but competition is keen, and you must be about early if you wish to get your share. Do not make a mistake when picking, and discard anything doubtful. It is not difficult to distinguish a mushroom from the various other fungi. Its outer surface is smooth, the underneath varies from pale pink to very dark brown, and the stalk is white. The feel is firm and fleshy, and should not be woody or wet to the touch.

You will probably notice mossy red and green balls on the twigs of the wild rose. They look like vegetable growths, but are really caused by the rose gall-wasp. These insects are smaller than house flies. The females lay their eggs in the shoots of the wild rose, causing them to swell and the mossy growth to form. It contains a hard core, in which are a number of separate cells, in each of which there is a grub and later a chrysalis.

The plough is now at work on the stubble fields.

Bird migration is in progress, but meanwhile those who intend to stay with us during the winter are making their preparations. The robins are fighting for their section of the garden and shrubbery. Once this is established, each will remain king over his own domain. Blackbirds and thrushes will return from the fields to the gardens a little later, when food becomes more scarce.

The swallows and house martins, which are the last of our summer visitors to leave, will be seen gathering in large numbers on telegraph wires and roofs as a preliminary to departure south.

The beautiful concentric webs of the spider attract attention, particularly in the morning, when each web is spangled with diamond-like globules of moisture.

Have you seen the skeins of gossamer carried by the wind? This is the young spider's method of seeking a new home. He usually ascends a tree and makes great lengths of gossamer, to which he clings when it floats away in the wind.

The vapourer moth is still plentiful. It is rather small—about one and a half inches across, but the single spot of clear white on each brown wing makes it easy to identify. The female is practically wingless.

The rather striking-looking caterpillar of the poplar hawk moth may now be discovered on the straight nibbled margins of the poplar leaves. It is yellowish green in colour, with a few narrow yellow lines and a hard horn-like growth at the back of the tail.

October

Ivy blossom is out. This is the last feast of the year for the insects, and attracts them by day and night.

Among the disappearing autumn flowers you may recognise the gipsywort, which still struggles bravely in moist ground. It has small white flowers on each stem, and a much broken up nettle-shaped leaf.

Another plant still in flower is the hemp agrimony. It grows by the stream side and in damp situations. The flowers are of a rather washed-out pink, and appear at the top of the rounded downy stem of the plant, which reaches a height of three to four feet.

The climbing corydalis is still showing white flowers tinged with delicate pink, which develop into pointed seed pods. Its brittle stems, clinging with sensitive tendrils, often grow to a great length.

The scarlet hips of the wild rose brighten the somewhat sombre lane sides. The haws, or hawthorn berries, are also a distinctive feature of the hedge. They will not remain for long, as they are an important item in the birds' menu. The missel-thrush in particular feeds greedily on them.

Magpies, which usually live in pairs, may sometimes at this season be seen in small flocks, as though assembling r migration. Food rather than travel is, however, their mediate object.

The greater plantain is still to be seen. It has broad, stalked leaves, and grows in large tufts on waste ground. The long seed spikes are used as food for cage birds. This plant differs from the ribwort plantain, which is such a pest on lawns, as the latter has narrow leaves.

During the summer the spindle tree is eclipsed in foliage and blossom by its neighbours, but the fruiting season has now arrived, and it comes into its own. The tree does not grow to any considerable size, and has a smooth olive-green bark, narrow leaves and small white flowers in May. In October the ripening seed becomes pinky orange, and the foliage a rich golden tint.

The last leaves, still green, are dropping from the ash trees, leaving the fruit hanging down in bundles, which remain until the spring winds scatter them. If you find an ash tree without these "bunches of keys" it is because it has borne male flowers only.

This is a period of autumn tints, and great patches of orange and brown make a pleasing contrast against the deeper green of the evergreens. Leaves are falling fast, and you will notice the walnut, horse-chestnut, sycamore and lime all have bare branches. The beech still carries its golden-brown leaves, and the elm is crowned with yellow.

The last of the summer birds, the swallows and martins, leave.

Young herons may be seen frequently at this time, as they seem to have less fear than their parents. In the case of the young heron, the facial stripe is grey instead of black, and the neck as yet unadorned by the long hanging plumes in front.

The crane-fly, or daddy-long-legs, is about in great numbers. To appreciate the reason for the incredib length of his legs, watch him walk over the top of long grass—an impossible feat were his legs shorter.

The dor-beetle can be seen, or more often heard, flying clumsily at night, after sleeping by day buried under the ground. He is violet blue in colour and oval in shape.

The satellite moth may be seen feeding on the ivy bloom. The fore wings are of a reddish brown, with or without a single white spot on each. The under wings are of a deep buff colour, the body stout and similar in colour to the fore wings.

November

Flowering plants are scarce, but the inconspicuous shepherd's purse continues to bloom. The small white flowers, without honey, are succeeded by curious heart-shaped seed pods.

Occasionally you will find some yellow flowers bearing an orange spot and resembling the garden snapdragon. This will be the toadflax, which continues to bloom sometimes up to Christmas.

Another flowering plant which may still be found is the scentless mayweed, which has white flowers with yellow centres, somewhat like daisies.

The ash, elm, poplar and hawthorn are now bare, but the oak still retains its leaves.

Catkins for next year may be seen forming on the hazel, alder and birch.

In the hedgerows and woods you may observe the small brilliant red berries of the wild arum. The leaves and outer cover have decayed, leaving the berries at the top of the short thick stalk.

The marble galls of the oak are of interest in a country-side which is settling down for its winter sleep. These

13

growths, which resemble marbles, are caused by a small black four-winged fly, which punctures the green twigs and deposits its eggs inside. For some unexplained reason, this causes the small round growths, in the centre of which the minute grub lives, feeds and finally changes to a chrysalis. When the insect emerges it bores its way out, leaving a small hole as evidence of its exit.

If you are lucky and observant, you may see a covey of partridges indulging in a dust bath in some secluded hollow. They do not use water for their ablutions, but indulge in these dust baths with great energy and enjoyment.

Goldfinches are feeding on the thistle seeds, for which their fine, pointed beaks seem specially suitable. Their black wings and tails are slightly marked with white and yellow. The underneath is fawn, and the head black and white marked with red.

This is a time when the common birds of prey are often seen. The peregrine falcon, monarch of his domain, can be located by the panic among the birds as they observe him, long before the human eye has picked up his solitary black figure in the sky. The kestrel is sometimes taken for the sparrow hawk, but can be easily distinguished, as the former has brown wings and is buff below, while the sparrow hawk has slate-grey wings and is a paler grey below. Their habits differ, as you may often see the kestrel hovering aloft watching the ground for some unwary mouse, while the sparrow hawk hunts the hedges and is difficult to detect; in fact, the small heaps of blood-stained feathers, the remains of his meal, are more frequently seen than the bird itself.

Common newts leave the water to hibernate at this time.

A few hardy butterflies and moths are hibernating, an

will appear next spring, when the warm weather awakens them from their winter sleep.

The winter moth is one of the few on the wing, and should be identified easily. The male is of a very deep buff or brown colour, the forewings being a darker shade than the under wings. The female is practically wingless, and can be observed on the trunks of fruit trees, where the caterpillars often do considerable damage in the spring.

The chestnut moth can also be seen. Its upper wings and body are yellowy brown, and the lower wings buff.

This is a good opportunity to discover some of the numerous varieties of land and water snails. Many of the land shells will be untenanted, their inhabitants having been eaten by ants and other scavengers. Take them home, wash and varnish them, and you will soon accumulate a most interesting and varied collection without the unpleasantness of killing and cleaning. The shells of the hedge snail are particularly fascinating, and even the common garden snail varies considerably.

December

The herons are early breeders, and are already beginning to take a vague interest in their nests. At a distance a heronry looks very much like a rookery, but on closer examination you will find the nests considerably larger than those of the rooks.

This is a month of few wild flowers. Here and there you will discover a gorse bush putting out a flash of yellow. The universal groundsel flowers on unperturbed by frost or bad weather, while chickweed and shepherd's purse complete the list. There is, however, hope of things to come; already the buds and leaves of the snowdrop are visible, and the more courageous spring plants are commencing to put out the tips of their leaves.

The common oak has divested itself of its leaves at last, but the evergreen oak, or ilex, provides a welcome touch of green in the landscape. Its leaves are long, narrow and pointed, and its acorns remain for weeks after those of the common oak have fallen and disappeared.

The cones of the pine, fir and larch can now be found.

You will notice a certain number of holly trees are without berries. They are the males, and the female trees only bear berries.

At this season the old dry flower heads of the teasel are conspicuous. If taken home and coloured, they make a very good decoration for Christmas.

You will notice those curious clusters of twigs on some trees forming tangled masses, which at first sight may be mistaken for birds' nests. These are known as "witches broom," and are caused by the attack of a minute fungus, which, like the gall fly, seems to possess the power of inducing excessive growth at the point of attack.

Bracken can be distinguished from all other British ferns by the fact that its fronds come out of the ground singly. By now it has changed to a rich golden yellow, and is an impressive sight when viewed in the mass from a distance.

The honeysuckle is exhibiting compact clusters of rich crimson berries.

The hedges are losing supplies of food berries, and birds are finding life more difficult.

Now the leaves have fallen, you will have an opportunity of examining nests which hitherto were out of sight. You will find some of them used as winter quarters by strangers. Sparrows may be in residence, or mice may use them as "dining tables," as will be seen by the nibbled remnants of many meals remaining.

Ash clusters, or ash galls, are small irregularly shape

lumps. They are really deformed female flowers which have turned black and become extremely hard through the attack of some microscopic insect.

The hawthorn sawfly has interesting winter quarters. Search the hawthorn carefully, and you may discover the extraordinary little box, under an inch in length, fixed tightly to the twigs. Inside this the sawfly sleeps the winter through, and emerges in early spring.

Chrysalids will come to light in strange places—under moss, under leaves, on tree trunks and buried beneath the dry grass clumps under the trees. In searching the ground you may come across a sleepy yellow caterpillar. This will be the larva of the cockchafer.

The December moth emerges this month. Its colour is subdued, consisting of two creamy yellow lines running across the fore wings of brownish purple. The hind wings are paler in colour, but carry a continuation of the yellow lines, and the fringes of the wings are chequered with yellow. This is one of those peculiar insects which some-times take one to two years to emerge from the chrysalis.

Have you discovered any fresh-water mussels? There are several varieties in old ponds and dykes. They measure from five inches in length in the case of the largest down to half an inch for the smallest kind.

Chapter VI

ARCHÆOLOGY AND ARCHITECTURE

Section 28

PREHISTORIC REMAINS

Barrows

The word "barrow" is occasionally applied to natural rises in the ground and to hillocks, but is used generally to denote a burial mound; usually raised artificially, but not always. It seems certain that from earliest times human beings were actuated by a common desire to honour the dead by raising some visible memorial to them. The custom of making mounds, or barrows as they are now called, was the outcome of this, and was characteristic of burials from most primitive times down to the eighth century. The practice was common with all races in all parts of the world; it is not suprising therefore that it was difficult to eradicate with the rise of Christianity, which demanded burial in cemeteries approved by the Church.

The primary idea was undoubtedly to provide a habitation for the dead, and therefore in its perfect form the barrow had one or more chambers, in which the dead rested with the possessions most prized when they were alive. The usual method was to rest the body in a doubled-up position, accompanied by weapons and implements of stone, and clay food and drinking vessels, not to be confused with the larger urns which were used sometimes to hold the cremated remains of the deceased.

The long barrow is characteristic of the Stone Age, an

usually contains one single chamber, entered by a passage which existed in the higher and wider end. However, it is impossible to determine definitely whether one or more chambers exist from an outside examination. This particular type of barrow is often of considerable length, and examples are still standing which measure over three hundred feet long by some sixty feet wide. Stones and earth were used in their construction, and although primitive, they were extremely strong. The chambers were made by overlapping the successive layers of the upper part of the side walls. In cases where these stone structures have been denuded of the earth covering, or no such covering existed, they are called "cromlechs." You will find large numbers still standing, composed of two or more unhewn stones set erect in the earth supporting a larger unhewn roof stone. A popular idea exists that these cromlechs were druidical altars, but it seems more likely that they are sepulchral remains.

The custom of cremation commenced in the Stone Age, before the long barrow had been discontinued. It is singular, however, that it appears to have been little used at that time in the south of England, and the majority of long barrows appear to be of the pre-cremation period, while the opposite seems to be the case in the north of England.

The bodies were usually burnt, and the remains enclosed in a big urn. It is not surprising, therefore, to find that with the new method of interment the size of the barrow decreased. As the chamber was no longer required as a habitation for the deceased, but merely to hold the urn, it was naturally made smaller, and the barrows became less and less imposing. This is typical of the Bronze Age, which succeeded the Stone Age. Those of the former are, however, extraordinarily rich in relics of their time, and ornaments of high artistic merit have been found frequently. In the succeeding Iron Age there appears to have been less uniformity in burial customs, although barrows in various forms still continued; they contained very often arms, accoutrements, and similar personal belongings.

Barrows usually occupy conspicuous sites, and frequently have an encircling ditch, or where the structure is stone, a low circle of stone. They are to be found all over Great Britain. The counties of Wiltshire and Dorset are particularly rich in these remains, and in these counties you may see mounds representing the Stone, Bronze and Iron Ages.

Section 29

ROMAN REMAINS

Although Julius Cæsar had visited Britain on two occasions, it was not until a century later that the Romans invaded and conquered the country. At first they subdued the south and midlands, but experienced considerable difficulty with the north and west. Final victory came about thirty years later after a long and bitter struggle. To defend the northern frontier, two defensive lines were constructed; first the massive permanent wall which exists to-day and is known as "Hadrian's Wall," from the name of the ruling Emperor at that time, and secondly a series of fortified posts stretching from the Forth to the Clyde.

Britain became a Roman province, and the large garrison, accompanied by their families, settlers and artisans, Romanised the country and introduced their culture and civilisation.

One of their most important works was the building of strategical roads, the chief characteristic of which was their amazing straightness. The Roman engineers constructed their roads in a straight line between the two required towns, and ignored or overcame natural obstacles. Some of these roads exist to-day; perhaps not complete, but always sufficiently to enable you to trace them out. Watling Street, The Icknield Way and the Fosse Way are all worth exploring.

The more important towns were well planned, with broad, paved streets running parallel and also crossing each other at right angles. They contained certain public buildings, among which was the basilica, or what might now be called the town hall, temples and public baths, and in some of the larger ones amphitheatres were built. Fine examples of Roman amphitheatres can be seen at Dorchester and Caerleon.

Houses and villas which have survived are mainly buried by the accumulated earth of centuries. The villas, or country residences, were substantially built on stone foundations, and had tiled roofs. They contained a number of rooms, and were heated by fires from below, which distributed the hot air through pottery pipes. They had very fine mosaic floors, or were often decorated with marble.

If you live near London, pay a visit to St. Albans, which is the site of the Roman city Verulamium. Here you will find remains of the old streets, villas and shops, and many articles of absorbing interest connected with the Roman occupation, which ended by the recall of the garrison when Rome herself was beset by enemies.

Section 30

CHURCH ARCHITECTURE

The history of a people is reflected in its ecclesiastical architecture. It is of course impossible in these brief notes to do more than give a few distinguishing features of the three early periods, Saxon, Norman and Gothic. Little remains of the Saxon; the Norman design died with the rise of Gothic, but the latter, although displaced at the end of the fifteenth century by the revival of the classic style, still had its adherents, and has remained in men's minds and influenced their design right up to the present century. Recently there seems a tendency to break away from the tradition of Gothic churches, and it is possible we are witnessing the commencement of a new era in style, which may well be as enduring as the great movements of the past.

It may be of interest, before proceeding to deal with our own churches, to consider very briefly the older continental styles, which had developed from the Greeks and Romans. Byzantine is the title applied to a particular form of architecture developed in Byzantium about A.D. 300. Its chief feature was the rise of the arch in place of the straight lintel, and the construction of a central dome carried by arches. The aisles were barrel vaulted, and the interior was decorated with marble and mosaics. If the inside was highly coloured, the brick exterior was simple in design, but of course surmounted by the central and subsidiary domes. Westminster Cathedral is one of the best examples of modern adaptation of Byzantine.

One more school of design might be considered for a moment, and that is Romanesque. It embraces all form of the round-arched Christian style, ending of cou

SAXON

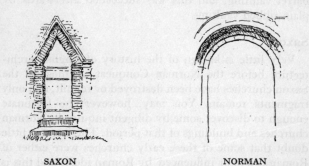

NORMAN

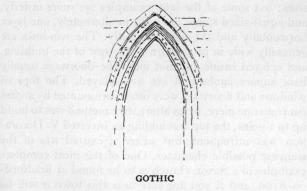

GOTHIC

with the introduction of Gothic. In its early stages a wooden roof was used, but later came the semicircular barrel vaulting, and this was succeeded afterwards by plain ribbed vaulting.

Saxon

Very little is known of the history of English architecture before the Norman Conquest, as most of the Saxon churches have been destroyed or rebuilt, and only fragments remain. You may, however, be fortunate enough to discover some by diligent inquiry in Norman churches and buildings of that period. There seems little doubt that some of these early churches were either of Roman origin or influenced by Roman ideas, and this is evident in the general design rather than in the materials or details of construction.

The general appearance of the stone work was uneven and loose jointed, sometimes the stone being of varying sizes; but some of the later examples are more orderly, and equal-sized stones are built in alternately, one layer horizontally and the next vertically. The windows are generally wide in proportion to the rest of the building, and splayed inside and not out. The doorways usually have square jambs and are not splayed. The tops of windows and doorways were often surmounted by arches cut from one piece, or an alternative method was to build up to a point, the top resembling an inverted V. Decoration was infrequent, but where it existed was of the simplest possible character. One of the most complete examples of a Saxon church is to be found at Bradford-on-Avon, and if you are ever near this town it will be worth while going some distance out of your way in order to view the little church.

Norman

The period of Norman architecture in England may be said to run from the Conquest, 1066, to the beginning of the development of Gothic, about 1200. At the time of the Conquest the Norman school of architectural thought was one of the most advanced in Europe. Although evolved from the Romanesque, it had a marked individuality of its own, which was soon impressed on conquered England. The Normans were not content with the small churches then common, but desired to erect monuments worthy of their conquest. As soon as they were safely settled, church, abbey and cathedral were rebuilt on a scale hitherto unknown in England, but at the same time many of the local peculiarities of the Saxons were retained.

The leading characteristics of the Norman style are size and massiveness. The doors and windows are simple, with semicircular arched heads; the latter without tracery. The nave arches are usually carried on massive pillars, and owing to the great size of the buildings, the architects were at first unable to vault the main roof, which was usually made of wood.

There are a number of Norman churches still in existence, and you should have no difficulty in recognising them if you bear in mind the above notes.

Gothic

The various styles of architecture which prevailed in Europe from the middle of the twelfth century to the revival of classic architecture at the beginning of the sixteenth century are termed " Gothic." This does not mean that the style was introduced by the Goths, but was bestowed by the Renaissance architects as a term of reproach. They held that their classic style was perfection, and that the new movement in the northern countries was barbarous and Gothic. The name has now outlived its original intention, and far from being regarded contemptuously, it is now considered one of the noblest styles ever invented.

The origin of Gothic is obscure, as it is not simply a logical development from earlier styles, but rather a spontaneous growth encouraged by a deep religious feeling which held the country. Feudalism was passing, and the people were awakening to a sense of national unity hitherto unknown. All art and all learning were centred on the Church. In it the divine, the painter, the sculptor and the mason all found scope for expression of their ideas. Gothic was probably first introduced into England during the rebuilding of Canterbury Cathedral, and from this it made rapid progress, impressed with the individuality of the English architects. The interesting point is that this style had a complete existence—it was born, reached maturity, and died. When the zeal of the early architects had exploited the design to its utmost limits, they rested on their labours, and their successors occupied themselves with details and the perfecting of every part. Finally, for the want of inspiration, the work passed into the hands of masons and craftsmen, perished, and was superseded by a revival of classic architecture. One of the most typical features of Gothic is the pointed arch, which superseded the round Norman arch.

The vaulting of the new design did not depend on massive walls and piers for support, but was stayed by flying buttresses, which were supported in turn by strong piers. Both the piers and buttresses were decorated by pinnacles, which to the uninitiated might give the impression of an excess of detail. In reality these arches, flying buttresses, were scientifically necessary, and integral part of the work. In other words, without them the fineness of the inside design would be impossible.

Gothic involved a breakaway from a massive and heavy appearance, and the substitution of something more delicate and subtle. The solid walls were now broken up, and occupied by more window than wall space. The supporting pillars were reduced in girth, and given a lightness of design which they had lacked hitherto, and the vaulting received similar treatment.

The progress of the Gothic was hastened by the introduction of stained glass. Hitherto churches had been decorated by wall paintings, but the brilliance of the little coloured pieces of glass held together by lead gave the inside of churches an appearance which fired the imagination. The very small pieces of stained glass were followed by larger pieces held together by lead, but even this improvement still left the churches very dark. The enlargement of windows followed, two or three being joined together. It was this desire for window space which was responsible for the delicate window tracery, which is such a striking feature of the style.

Wood carvers and sculptors also devoted their work to the churches. Large numbers of statues were carved and used as decorations both inside and out.

There are many other features which might be discussed if space permitted, but sufficient has been said to give a broad idea of what Gothic is and how this great legacy came to us.

In wandering through England you will find it is the favourite style for ecclesiastic architecture, and many modern churches bear its imprint.

Section 31

CASTLES

The first castles, designed for residence as well as defence, may be said to have been introduced by the Normans after the Conquest. It is true the Romans designed a form of armed encampment, but this was not designed for residence; and it is equally true that some of the more important Saxon landowners fortified their houses in a primitive way, but by no stretch of imagination could they be termed castles. The most that can be said for Saxon fortification is that certain towns were walled, and even so, many of the walls were of Roman origin. The absence of strongholds may well be the reason why the Normans found the Conquest comparatively simple, and possibly the building of castles followed as a protective measure against the resentment which naturally followed the change. As the castles grew in size and strength by the improvements and additions of succeeding generations, they gave their possessors not only security from their neighbours, but a certain independence of the central government. It is no exaggeration to say that these strongholds had a profound effect upon the history of England.

The general plan of the castle was as follows. A wooden structure, usually a tower, called the "keep," was erected on top of the large central mound of earth, and this was surrounded by a stockade and wide ditch. Below the mound and adjacent was the court, or bailey; this in turn was protected by its own ditch and stockade. In some cases ramparts, protected by another ditch, would surround both mound and bailey.

In the later castles, the keep was constructed of sto

crowned by battlements, and the entrance gates were watched by stone towers. Entry was obtained by means of a wooden drawbridge, and the huge wooden gates had the additional protection of a portcullis, which was dropped down in grooves in the masonry.

Inside the bailey, which was sometimes divided into several courts, were the barracks, chapel, stables and other buildings. These were nearly always made of wood, and in the course of time have disappeared. In examining castles to-day, you must bear this fact in mind in order to visualise them as they were.

The keep was more strongly defended than any other part of the fortress, and was designed to give the garrison a final chance if driven from the outer defences. It contained a well, in case of siege, a chapel, and all the other requirements of residence and defence, and last, but not least, the dungeons below. The best-known example of a keep is at Windsor Castle, and this must be familiar to a great many readers.

The sites of castles varied. High ground suggested itself, but often this was out of the question owing to the lack of a good water supply. As this was before the days of gunpowder, it was not essential to choose a position which was not overlooked by higher ground, and many castles were built on the sides of rivers, which gave protection on one side. In addition, water was plentiful both for drinking and to fill the moat. The essence of the whole structure was the maximum strength obtained with the minimum number of men.

As the years passed by the times became more settled, and further improvements were made; keeps were constructed entirely of stone, and the stockades were replaced by stone ramparts. Castles built about this time were entirely of stone, and the central keep was usually a vast

4

square tower with an outer courtyard protected by ramparts and a moat.

The decline of the castle was brought about by two factors. First, the introduction of artillery rendered their passive defence more difficult; and secondly, as they were not required for defensive purposes, the discomfort of life within encouraged people to construct their dwellinghouses outside.

Chapter VII

Section 32

HOBBIES

COLLECTION AND PAINTING OF FIR CONES,
LEAVES AND TWIGS FOR HOME DECORATION

How many of you who bemoan the falling of those wonderful golden-yellow beech leaves in the autumn, realise that they may be preserved for a long period if treated with colourless varnish? First obtain permission, and then cut small branches of suitable size, making sure that the leaves are not too far advanced and will not fall before you reach home. Lay each branch in turn on a newspaper spread on the floor, and paint over every leaf, stem and branch with a good quality colourless varnish, using a soft brush which has been soaked in water for some hours previously. Hang up for some days to dry in a dustless room, and you will have a most attractive form of decoration for some time.

Another idea used widely is to cut evergreens, preferably laurels, because their big shiny leaves are particularly suitable for the purpose, and paint them over with silver or golden paint, leaving the stems green. Some people think the result rather artificial, but in the dark evenings, and particularly at Christmas, they form a very welcome addition to the few forms of decoration available.

Another variation is to cut rather long leafless twigs and to paint them irregularly with gold or silver.

Fir cones can be collected in autumn and dried over

the winter. In this process they open, and if painted with some of the glossy enamels now available, fill the empty fireplace most effectively, when fires cease in the following spring. As an alternative, the cones may be painted silver and gold, and suspended as a form of hanging decoration.

You may think these ideas crude, but if carried out artistically, they can be very attractive.

WALKING-STICKS FROM THE WOODS AND LANES

Every one uses a walking-stick at some time, and although they may be bought quite cheaply, it is interesting to cut and make them yourself, taking care not to destroy the hedges.

Cut in the winter, because the sap is not rising and the absence of leaves will make your choice easier. The sticks should be of a suitable length and thickness. They should be several inches longer than required, to allow for the handle and to permit cutting away if a split occurs in the drying process.

Any odd small twigs should not be cut off at this stage, but left until dry.

To dry and straighten, hang up for six months by the thick end with a weight attached to the thin end.

When this process is finished, cut off the twigs, and if the bark is to be removed, soak the stick in hot water and rub down with a piece of sacking or similar rough material.

Treat the handle by putting the stick in boiling water for fifteen minutes, and then gently and slowly bend the wood as desired. If you prefer, this operation can be performed over steam. Tie the handle in position by strong, smooth string to prevent it straightening. Having done this, suspend by the handle with a weight at the other end.

When dry, file down any knobs and scrape with broken

glass, then use fine and coarse glass-paper to smooth. Wipe clear of all dust, and varnish with best carriage varnish, having previously put in a tack at the bottom to suspend the stick in a dustless place for drying. When dry, wipe over carefully with powder pumice stone, just sufficient to dull the surface. Clean and apply a second coat of varnish. Your stick will then be ready, except for the ferrule, which can be purchased locally for a few coppers. Any colour or stain should be applied before the varnish.

A straight stick or staff is very effective if the end is carved carefully, but be sure to cut up and not down the grain.

Willow, sycamore, oak, holly, wild cherry, crab, blackthorn, yew, maple, ash and hazel are all good, but ash, blackthorn and elm are best cut from saplings.

ELDERBERRY WINE

Wait until the elderberries are ripe, and gather on a dry day. Pick off the stalks, clean and bruise the berries, and pour one gallon of boiling water on to each one and a half gallons of fruit. Let this stand for twenty-four hours, stirring occasionally.

Draw off the liquor, strain it and add three and a half pounds of sugar for every gallon of fruit used. Boil for fifteen minutes, carefully skimming meanwhile.

At this stage draw off the wine into a cask and allow to cool. When it is about seventy to seventy-five degrees, put in some yeast on toast. This will ferment, and during the process add cloves, ginger and spices to taste. When fermentation has ceased, bung up the cask, and bottle after three months.

DANDELION WINE

Place four quarts of dandelion heads into a clean tub. Boil one gallon of water, allow it to stand until lukewarm, and pour over the dandelions. Stir well, cover up and leave for four or five days, continuing to stir at frequent intervals.

Strain off into a pan, add three and a half pounds of lump sugar, one ounce ground ginger, one orange and one lemon sliced together with their chopped-up rinds. Boil for half an hour, then when lukewarm add a slice of toast covered with yeast. Cover up again for a few days, strain into a cask and leave for three months before bottling.

Cowslip wine can be made in the same way.

Chapter VIII

FIELD PHOTOGRAPHY

The Camera

Your choice of camera will depend upon the use you intend to make of it. Obviously the same camera will not be suitable for small snapshots of friends, the rapid movement of a horse or hare in action or the carefully prepared study of a bird on her nest. Considerations of price and cost of upkeep are also rather important for many of us.

For beginners and those who merely wish to record the events of a happy holiday, the box camera is perhaps the best. These box cameras are cheap, and simple in construction and working. They take a roll of films of standard size which can be purchased anywhere; spare rolls can be carried in the pocket and changed by daylight.

If this is your standard of photography, and incidentally you will get a good deal of amusement from it, you will probably not worry to develop your own films or make your own prints. Select a reliable photographic dealer or chemist, and he will be able to advise you on your mistakes.

Small, low-priced cameras of the folding type are made, but for general purposes the box camera is to be preferred. The former possess one advantage only, and that is they can be carried in the pocket.

Later on you may wish to take fast-moving objects, and for this purpose the reflex or press camera is the only possibility. It is expensive, and you are not recommended to invest in one of this type until you are experienced. However, if you pursue the study and your pocket is sufficiently deep, you will find a reflex of extraordinary interest and with immense possibilities.

If you propose to try your skill at field photography, a quarter-plate tripod focusing camera of the bellows variety is the only possibility. They may be purchased new or second-hand, but if the latter, be sure and go to a reliable dealer. These cameras hold plates, which, although more difficult to change in the field, are easier to handle and develop at home.

The lens is of importance; in the cheaper cameras these are standard and of good value, but it is an obvious advantage in field work to use a movable lens for focusing your object. Such a lens will be provided with your bellows camera.

Within the limit of these brief notes it is not possible to go into the details of anastigmatic lenses, the knowledge of and proper use of the focal length of your lens, the problems of the shutter, and the hundred and one technicalities which will occur to the mind of the expert. You will learn a certain amount from a good text-book, and a great deal more from experience.

We will assume that you have now bought your camera, and with dark slides loaded with plates are going out in search of "game." By the way, you will find "hunting with the camera" one of the finest of all sports. The possibilities are enormous; you may collect birds, beasts, flowers, insects, or what you will, but it is all accomplished without cruelty or destruction. In fact, even from the collector's point of view, photography has many advantages over the mere accumulation of specimens.

A bird's egg in a box is a trifle dull, but a photograph of the clutch in the nest, with perhaps another of the mother bird, and finally a picture of the general surroundings of the nest, give a record with which the solitary egg cannot compare. In addition, remember you have all the excitement of the find and the patient stalking to obtain your objective. It is impossible to preserve fungi, but a photographic collection of them is not difficult to obtain. Tree photography is an attractive study. Take and collect a series of trees in summer with their full canopy of leaves; in the winter take the same trees from a similar position. The comparison between two such photographs is most instructive and full of interest.

In winter, frost photography will supply you with some amazing results. To obtain the best effects, you must be about early, before the wintry sun dulls the effect of the overnight transformation. Good results can be obtained from frosted foliage, and in general the nearer you can approach your object, the more satisfied you will be with the picture. Trees are sometimes disappointing, particularly if taken against a blue background of sky.

You may wish to photograph wild flowers, and the summer months certainly give wide opportunities for this fascinating work, although you will probably have a number of disappointments at first. You will find that snapshot work rarely gives the best results, and that a long exposure is necessary, after which the plates should be developed with a dilute solution of developer; the object being to bring out the texture of the flower with a soft effect rather than a hard, brittle appearance. You will remember this hint of dilute developer when dealing with cloud negatives. Cloud studies are worth trying. You will lose a few pictures by trial and error, but the resulting knowledge will enable you to get something worth keeping.

In photographing flowers and other small objects, you

will find a tilting table necessary. This can be bought for a few shillings, or made at home, as it is quite simple. Two pieces of flat wood about six inches by four inches are hinged together on one side. The lower piece has a hole to admit the tripod screw, and the upper a hole to admit the camera screw. A wooden wedge is placed between the two pieces of wood to alter the angle of the camera, and this works satisfactorily until you move it round at right angles to the ground; a piece of thin wire attached to the ends will prevent them opening too widely, or going beyond ninety degrees. The advantage of such a table is clear, as with the aid of a short tripod you can get your object at any angle.

The tilting table is not advised for fungi, as they are so low that if taken from an angle they will appear distorted, and the head will be out of proportion to the stem. The best plan is to use a "baby tripod," which will necessitate you kneeling or lying on the ground. Under-exposure is the usual fault with this form of work, and therefore err on the side of extra time.

Having graduated with still life, you will become more ambitious and wish to try your luck with birds. You will be embarking on an adventurous time. We leave the question of taking the rook and the heron high up in the trees, because when you reach this stage you will have developed a technique of your own.

Consider first the nests on ground-level. The important thing here is to get your camera as near the ground as possible. Obviously it must be raised about a foot, but no more.

For the song-birds and those breeding in bushes and hedgerows, rules are difficult if not impossible, because each case will present its own problems. Do not disturb the site or cut away branches; if absolutely necessary hold or tie them back. If you are taking eggs, it is better as a rule to show two or three only, and leave the rest hidden by the cup-shaped formation of the nest. The camera should not look directly down but along the object.

The real difficulties commence when you attempt to take the parent birds. Most observers have noticed that birds which build their nests in hedges and similar places have some point to which they fly before entering the nest. A little watching will enable you to find this point, which may possibly be a small twig or stump. Once this outlook point is established, the procedure is easy.

When the bird has left its nest in search of food, focus your camera on the tree or stump, and cover it with a piece of canvas coloured brown or green, or with pieces of twig. Run out a long piece of rubber tube with a bulb on the end to work your shutter. This tube should be about forty feet in length. Now retire to the best hiding-place you can find within range of your tubing, and wait until the bird returns, and squeeze the bulb the moment it alights. Wait until it flies away again before changing your plate for a second attempt. Another method is to work the shutter by means of a dry battery, switch and electric wire. If you are electrically minded, you will find this simple, but if you have no knowledge of electricity, leave this idea alone.

Finally, there is the method of the hide. The general principle is to secrete yourself and camera under suitably coloured canvas and wait. Various ideas exist, the most general of which is a framework of laths, round which the canvas may be tied. Holes are made one end for the watcher and his camera. Birds are, however, very suspicious, and if it is possible to leave your hide in position for a few days before using, a great deal of time may be saved.

There remain a large number of subjects on which we have not been able to touch, but you will choose your own, and whatever the choice, you will find the result absorbing and of ever-increasing interest.

You will probably want to develop your own plates sooner or later. Many are deterred from doing so by the supposed difficulty of finding a suitable place. The bath-room can be converted conveniently by making a wooden frame, covered with dark material, which will fit over the window. This can be put up and removed in a few seconds, and, as an additional precaution, only work after dark.

The ruby lamp can be of an expensive variety, but you will find one of the ordinary oil type quite satisfactory if an electric torch is substituted for the oil lamp.

A small cupboard for your chemicals and dishes and a table for the operation should be provided. If space is restricted, a piece of board over the basin makes a very satisfactory substitute.

After exposing the plate in the camera, an invisible image is formed on the plate. This image is made visible by the process of developing, and a negative is obtained, from which the print or positive is afterwards made.

The negative depends mainly on two things, the ex-posure given the plate when in the camera and the developing process. There is a minimum exposure for every plate, and if it has not received this, no amount of developing will produce a satisfactory result. There is also a maximum exposure, beyond which it is unsafe to go. Various aids to determine exposure are sold in the shape of cards and meters, but the most satisfactory of all is experience, and a few failures will teach you a tremendous amount if you think.

There are many different kinds of developer, and in

the early stages it would be wise to consult your photographic dealer as to the best for the type of plate being used. Later you will master the intricacies of various makes and choose for yourself.

After development, it is necessary to what is called "fix" the negatives, that is, prevent further chemical action taking place. This is done by placing them in a saturated solution of hypo. The crystals are bought at the chemist's for a few coppers, and the solution made up in a big bottle. Dissolve as many of the crystals as the water will take, some time before using.

After fixing, the negatives are washed in running water for an hour to remove all traces of chemical, and dried in a dust-free room by standing up vertically.

When dry, you may obtain your print by placing the negative in a printing frame over a piece of daylight printing paper. The positive will slowly appear on the paper, and when it is a little darker than the tone finally required, it should be plunged into a toning bath, which stays all further action.

There is another method which is useful, and that is gaslight paper. The paper is inserted in the frame behind the negative in the same way as before, and held about eighteen inches in front of an electric or gas light for a few moments. It shows no sign of the picture at this stage, but when plunged into a developing solution, the image appears rapidly. When developed, it is placed in a fixing bath and washed in the same way as a negative.

Chapter IX

Section 34

GAMES FOR THE RAMBLER

Ring Tennis

Apparatus: a piece of string or tape, and a rope or rubber ring, obtainable at any sports dealer's.

The string is stretched across on two sticks, as a substitute for a net, and the game is played on similar lines to lawn tennis, except that the ring is used instead of a ball, and the hands instead of racquets.

Neither in playing or serving may the ring be above the level of the player's shoulders as it leaves his hand.

The server hurls the ring over the tape to his opponent, who catches it and returns it immediately to the other side of the net.

If a player fails to catch the ring, or allows it to touch the ground, he loses the point as he would in tennis if he missed the ball or struck it on the second bounce.

In serving, if the ring passes beneath the tape, it is a fault, and a second fault is against the server.

The remaining rules are as for tennis.

Conjure or Tip-Cat Cricket

A game for eight or more players. Obtain two stout sticks about three feet long, and a small stick or tip cat which has been trimmed slightly at each end and is about six inches long. Mark two circles of about a foot in diameter distinctly with the ends of the tip cat, about four paces apart. Divide sides and toss for innings.

The opening players take their places with the ends

their sticks resting inside the circles. A server stands behind each circle, and the remaining members of the fielding side take their places in the field.

The tip cat is then served with the object of placing it inside the striker's circle. If the latter hits it, he may or may not run to the opposite circle, and his partner runs in the reverse direction, for as many times as they think safe. A player may be run out by the tip cat being placed inside the circle before the end of his striking stick is home. If as a result of a service the tip cat falls inside the circle, the striker is out, but if it falls on the line marking the circumference, a "conjure" is made, and the two servers retire and secrete the tip cat on them, returning with their hands either in their sleeves or coat and kneeling by the circle at either end. The strikers now have to change ends without the tip cat being placed in the circle while they are running and putting them out, or, in other words, being stumped. Practice will teach you to form a very good idea at which end the tip cat is hidden, and the player from the opposite end, by running down quickly before his partner moves away, may effect the change without either being put out.

All the other rules are as for cricket.

Chapter X

Section 35

DIRECTORY OF CLUBS AND ASSOCIATIONS

The Camping Club of Great Britain and Ireland, 38, Grosvenor Gardens, London, S.W.1

Fosters the sport of camping and brings together people interested in the open air. Protects the interests of campers against restrictive legislation. Requires all members to undertake to carry out the Campers' Code. Issues a monthly journal to all members, and publishes the "Handbook on Camping," also free, to members. This is the acknowledged authority on the technical side of the sport. Supplies a list of camping sites, and maintains certain permanent camping grounds of its own. Members can obtain preferential terms for purchase of kit, insurance, railway fares, etc. Special sections exist for the benefit of those interested in canoeing, mountaineering and caravanning. Annual subscriptions: Full Members, 10/-; Associate Members, 5/-; Family Members, 2/6. Entrance fee, 1/-. Small additional subscriptions for special sections: Canoeing, 5/-; Mountaineering, 5/-; Caravanning, 2/6.

The Ramblers' Association, 7, Buckingham Palace Gardens, London, S.W.1

Protects the interests of ramblers and maintains and extends their rights and privileges. Encourages rambling and fosters a greater love and knowledge of the countryside. Maintains friendly relations with landowners and the rural community generally; assists in the preservation of the countryside. The Association secures special travelling facilities for ramblers, and acts as a bureau of information for its members in regard to catering, sleeping accommodation, routes, maps and equipment. Annual subscriptions: Associate Members, 2/6; societies not exceeding 50, 7/6; over 50 members but not exceeding 200, 15/–; exceeding 200 members, 22/6. Publishes an annual handbook and directory. Hon. General Secretary: G. R. Mitchell, 7, Buckingham Palace Gardens, London, S.W.1.

DISTRICT FEDERATIONS
Hon. Secretaries

Cumberland . .	Roland Taylor, Glendermott, Loop Road North, Whitehaven.
Lancashire, North-East . . .	L. Mills, 47, Longton Street, Blackburn.
Leicestershire .	F. H. Southorn, 230, Hinckley Road, Leicester.
Lincolnshire .	N. A. Rushworth, 92, Scarthoe Road, Grimsby.
Liverpool . .	W. S. Tysoe, 14, Cambridge Chambers, 77a, Lord Street, Liverpool, 2.
Manchester .	Miss N. Willington, 14, Ridgefield, John Dalton Street, Manchester.
Midland . .	F. E. Ritchie, 16, Clarendon Road, Edgbaston, Birmingham.
Northern . . .	K. Wilson, Roachburn, Stamfordham Road, Newcastle-on-Tyne.
Nottingham and Derbyshire	F. J. E. Young, 98, Broxtowe Lane, Cinderhill, Nottingham.

Sheffield . . .	S. E. Morton, 2, Barnt Road, Bent Green, Sheffield.
Southern . . .	G. R. Mitchell, 7, Buckingham Palace Gardens, London, S.W.1.
Staffordshire, North . . .	D. Griffin, 11, Victoria Place, Penkhull, Stoke-on-Trent.
West of England .	H. Overton, B.Sc., 447, St. John's Lane, Bristol, 3.
Yorks, West Riding	Miss L. Robinson, 283, Aireville Mt., Frizinghall, Bradford.
South Wales . .	L. C. Josty, 58, Neville Street, Cardiff.
Scottish Ramblers' Federation . .	Gen. Secretary: J. Snedden, 66, Kildonan Street, Coatbridge, Glasgow.

The Royal Photographic Society, 35, Russell Square, London, W.C.1

Exists to promote the general advancement of photography and its applications. Arranges meetings from October to May, and holds exhibitions throughout the year. Has a library, dark rooms and workroom available for members. Publishes the *Photographic Journal* monthly. Entrance fee: 1 guinea. Annual membership: 2 guineas, with nominal additional subscriptions to the various specialised groups.

The Roads Beautifying Association, 7, Buckingham Palace Gardens, London, S.W.1

Exists to promote the planting and beautifying of the highways of this country. Has formed a central voluntar body of experts who give their services in inspecti the miles of new arterial roads and advising on the planting and maintenance of trees. Annual subscription: 1 guinea.

The Pedestrians' Association, 3, Tudor Street, London, E.C.4

Formed to promote and preserve the safety and amenity of public highways in the interests of all persons using them, particularly persons on foot. The Association is not a Rambling Club, although many ramblers are members, as are many cyclists and motorists. Ensures that the views of pedestrians are fully stated and their needs adequately met in all questions as to use of highways and the control of traffic. Gives free legal advice to members injured while using the roads afoot. Annual subscription: Any sum from 2/6.

The Holiday Fellowship, Fellowship House, Great North Way, Hendon, N.W.4

Provides guest-houses and camps, and organises holidays amid many of the finest scenes in Britain and abroad. Provides at its guest-houses local guides and organises daily excursions under expert leadership to places of beauty and historical and cultural interest in the district. It encourages tramping on mountain, coast and moorland, and provides accommodation at most reasonable rates. Arranges an exchange of visits between members of different nationalities. It is more than a travel association, and seeks to stimulate the social instincts of its members and provides genial companionship for those who are compelled to take their holidays independently of their friends. Owns an international guest-house, standing in seven acres of ground at Hitherwood, 19, Sydenham Hill, S.E.26.

Youth Hostels Association, 18, Bridge Road, Welwyn Garden City, Herts

Encourages young people to walk and cycle over the countryside, and aims at providing cheap and simple accommodation for both sexes in a large number of hostels, the addresses of which are given to members. The charge is 1/– per night for bed and blankets, and members carry their own sleeping-bags. Cooking facilities are provided for those who wish to cook their own meals, but others can obtain food at specially low prices. The work of the Association goes far beyond the provision of hostels, as it seeks to improve the body and mind by engendering a love for fresh air and the open country. Non-political and non-sectarian, it works for the preservation of the countryside and a return to simpler standards of living, and finally for the freedom of youth and a better understanding between young people of all classes and nationalities. Subscriptions: 5/– per annum, or 2/6 if under twenty-five years of age.

The National Cyclists' Union, 35, Doughty Street, London, W.C.1

Provides free insurance against claims by third parties arising out of accidents whilst riding or wheeling a cycle. Free legal advice in support of just claims arising from cycling. Issues a touring handbook, giving the addresses of hotels, inns and boarding-houses which have been approved by the Union. Gives free advice and information on touring at home and abroad. Special rates for insurance of bicycles and riders, and numerous other advantages. No entrance fee. Annual subscription, 6/6, but reduced rates for families.

The Cyclists' Touring Club, 3, Craven Hill, London, W.C.2

Publishes cycling literature, including first-class road books and the yearly handbook containing the addresses of approved hotels, farmhouses and other suitable quarters. Issues a monthly magazine to members. Gives free insurance against third-party risks, including road racing. Renders public service to cyclists by the promotion of legislation in Parliament in the interests of cyclists. Has representatives in all principal towns, both at home and on the Continent. Supplies information for tourists, and a special Customs ticket for the admission of a cycle to certain European countries. Entrance fee, 1/–. Annual subscription, 10/–. Reduction for family membership.

The Royal Society for the Protection of Birds, 82, Victoria Street, London, S.W.1

Encourages the better preservation of wild birds. Promotes research and study in all matters connected with birds by means of exhibitions, lectures, meetings and literature. Provides or assists other societies to provide watches for the protection of wild birds in certain localities. Annual subscriptions: Fellow, from 21/–; Member, from 5/–; Associate, from 1/–.

The Commons, Open Spaces and Footpaths Preservation Society, 71, Eccleston Square, Victoria, London, S.W.1

Objects: To preserve for the benefit of the public all commons and open spaces; to secure and maintain the free and uninterrupted use of all public rights of way by land and water; to prevent the abuse of public rights and privileges, especially trespass, damage to wild flowers, crops and game, and the litter nuisance; to secure the provision of finger-posts and suitable stiles on footpaths. Minimum annual subscription: 10/6 for Members, and 5/– for Associate members.

The Royal Life Saving Association, 8, Bayley Street, London, W.C.1

Promotes technical education in life-saving and re-suscitation of the apparently drowned. Encourages floating, diving, plunging and such other swimming arts as would be of assistance to a person endeavouring to save life. Arranges public lectures, demonstrations, competitions and classes of instruction. Publishes a comprehensive handbook of instruction. Subscription for individual membership, 2/6; for clubs, 10/6 per annum.

The Men of the Trees, 10, Victoria Street, Westminster, S.W.1

A voluntary society of Tree Lovers, who are working to create a universal tree-sense and encourage all to plant, protect and love trees. Founded by Richard St. Barbe Baker among the tribesmen of Kenya, in order to save their land from barrenness resulting from the thoughtless destruction of forests, the Society has grown world wide and is pledged to the cause of trees, whether these be grown for timber, for ornament, for fruit or for shade. Among its activities, the Men of the Trees has periodical meetings, excursions, tree photographic competitions, picture exhibitions and lantern lectures. Issues an Annual Report and Review of the Tree Year. Annual subscription, 5/–, or 7/6 to include the Society's journal, Trees, which deals with trees in their literary, historical, æsthetic and practical aspects. The Tree Badge, sent to all on joining, serves as an introduction to those for whom trees have an instinctive appeal.

The National Trust, 7, Buckingham Palace Gardens, Westminster, S.W.1

Founded in 1895 for the purpose of promoting the permanent preservation for the benefit of the nation, of lands and buildings of beauty or historic interest, and, as regards lands, for the preservation, as far as practicable, of their natural features, animal and plant life.

The Scapa Society, 71, Eccleston Square, London, S.W.1

Founded in 1893 for the purpose of protecting the picturesque simplicity of rural and river scenery, and to promote a due regard for dignity and propriety of aspect in towns; with special reference to the abuses of spectacular advertising. To assist generally the national importance of maintaining the elements of interest and beauty in out-of-door life. To combat the nuisance caused by the scattering of litter.

The Council for the Preservation of Rural England, 4, Hobart Place, London, S.W.1

Co-ordinates the efforts of many national associations, institutes and societies, each of which is interested in preserving rural scenery from some special danger, or in protecting the artistic and historic features of country towns and villages. It does not object to the reasonable use and development of rural areas, but to the abuse and bad development of such areas.

The Wayfaring Association of Great Britain, 4, Heugh Street, Falkirk, Scotland

Members have full use of the Service Bureau, and advice is given free on all wayfaring matters. Itineraries at home and abroad and guide books for any district are supplied free, passports obtained, travel tickets purchased, and accommodation reserved for members without fee. A complete library of maps covering the rambling grounds of Europe is available. Annual subscription, 5/–. $2\frac{1}{2}$ per cent. reduction on all Tours organised by the Association.

The Climbers' Club, 31, Helenslea Avenue, London, N.W.11

Founded in 1897, to encourage rock climbing and hill walking; and to inculcate a love of the hills and fells; to further the interests of science and art in relation thereto. Has a Club Cottage on the Capel Curig–Bangor Road, for the use of members at a nominal charge. Entrance fee, 1 guinea; annual subscription, 1 guinea.

Chapter XI

Section 36

BIBLIOGRAPHY

*The title of the work is given first and then the author's name.
The publisher is given in italics*

BIRDS

Birds of the British Isles and their Eggs. T. A. Coward.
F. Warne & Co.

Birds' Eggs and Nests. S. N. Sedgwick. *The Epworth
Press.*

Birds Shown to the Children. *T. C. and E. C. Jack, Ltd.*

Nests and Eggs Shown to The Children. *T. C. and E. C.
Jack, Ltd.*

British Birds; Their Nests and Eggs. W. M. Gallichan.
Holden and Hardingham.

FLOWERS

Wayside and Woodland Blossoms (3 Vols.). Edward
Step. *F. Warne & Co.*

Flowers Shown to the Children. *T. C. and E. C. Jack,
Ltd.*

Wild Flowers. Hilderic Friend. *The Epworth Press.*

Wild Flowers. MacGregor Skene. *T. Nelson & Sons.*

Wild Flowers and How To Know Them at a Glance.
Col. J. S. F. Mackenzie. *Holden and Hardingham.*

Botanical Names of Wild Flowers, What They Mean and
How Pronounced. Col. J. S. F. Mackenzie. *Holden
and Hardingham.*

TREES

Wayside and Woodland Trees. Edward Step. *F. Warne & Co*.

Woodland Trees. J. H. Crabtree. *The Epworth Press*.

Trees Shown to the Children. *T. C. and E. C. Jack, Ltd*.

Among the Trees. R. St. Barbe Baker. *The Men of the Trees*.

British Trees and How to Name Them at a Glance. Foster Robson. *Holden and Hardingham*.

FERNS

Wayside and Woodland Ferns. Edward Step. *F. Warne & Co*.

British Ferns. J. H. Crabtree. *The Epworth Press*.

BUTTERFLIES, MOTHS AND INSECTS

Butterflies of the British Isles. Richard South. *F. Warne & Co*.

Moths of the British Isles (2 Vols.). Richard South. *F. Warne & Co*.

Butterflies. S. N. Sedgwick. *The Epworth Press*.

Moths of the Months. S. N. Sedgwick. *The Epworth Press*.

Butterflies Shown to the Children. *T. C. and E. C. Jack, Ltd*.

Insects Shown to the Children. *T. C. and E. C. Jack, Ltd*.

British Insects. J. H. Crabtree. *The Epworth Press*.

Beetles and Spiders. S. N. Sedgwick. *The Epworth Press*.

ANIMALS

Animal Life of the British Isles. Edward Step. *F. Warne & Co.*

British Wild Animals, Their Tracks and Habits. H. Mortimore Batten. *C. Arthur Pearson, Ltd.*

English Wild Animals. J. F. Blakesborough. *Burns Oates.*

ARCHITECTURE

Architecture Shown to the Children. *T. C. and E. C. Jack, Ltd.*

The Development of the Castle. *The Historical Association.*

The English Parish Church. Samuel Gardiner. *The Historical Association.*

The Parish Churches of England. J. C. Cox. *Batsford.*

CAMPING

Standing Camps. D. Frances Morgan. *Boy Scouts' Association.*

Tramp Camping. W. L. Pember. *Ernest Benn.*

Hiking. D. Frances Morgan. *C. Arthur Pearson, Ltd.*

FIRST AID

First Aid to the Injured. *St. John Ambulance Association.*

MISCELLANEOUS

In Nature's Ways. Marcus Woodward. *C. Arthur Pearson, Ltd.*

Natural History of Selborne. Gilbert White. *Everyman's Library.*

Wild Fruits and How to Know Them. Stanley C. Johnson. *Holden and Hardingham*.

Grasses and Rushes and How to Know Them. Stanley C. Johnson. *Holden and Hardingham*.

How to Forecast the Weather. Joseph H. Elgie. *Holden and Hardingham*.

Handbook of Instruction. *The Royal Life Saving Society*.

INDEX

INDEX

231

NOTES

NOTES

NOTES

NOTES

NOTES

NOTES

PRINTED IN GREAT BRITAIN BY WILLIAM CLOWES AND SONS, LIMITED,
LONDON AND BECCLES.